BACKROAD WINER
SOUTHERN CALIFORNIA

A SCENIC TOUR OF CALIFORNIA'S COUNTRY WINERIES

Written and Photographed by Bill Gleeson

CHRONICLE BOOKS

SAN FRANCISCO

ABOUT THE AUTHOR

Bill Gleeson is a fourth-generation Californian who grew up traveling the back roads of the Central Valley and the gold country. Gleeson's lifelong interest in the roads less traveled has led to the publication of several other books. These include a companion book, *Backroad Wineries of Northern California* (1994), as well as the popular *Weekends for Two* series of romantic getaway guides to Northern California, Southern California, and the Pacific Northwest. All are published by Chronicle Books.

A graduate of California State University, Chico, Gleeson lives with his wife, Yvonne, and children, Kari and Jeff, in the Northern California foothills.

All photographs and maps by Bill Gleeson

Copyright ©1994 by Bill Gleeson.

Printed in Hong Kong.

Book and cover design: William Reuter Design

Library of Congress Cataloging-in-Publication Data

Gleeson, Bill.
    Backroad wineries of southern California: a scenic tour
of California's country wineries / Bill Gleeson.
        p. cm.
    Includes index.
    ISBN 0-8118-0335-X
    1. Wine and wine making—California, Southern. I. Title.
    II. Title: Backroad wineries of southern California.
TP557.G585 1994
641.2'2'097941—dc20   93-31266
                                                             CIP

Distributed in Canada by Raincoast Books,
112 East Third Avenue, Vancouver, B.C. V5T 1C8

10 9 8 7 6 5 4 3 2 1

Chronicle Books
275 Fifth Street
San Francisco, CA 94103

Oh, for a draught of vintage that hath been
Cool'd a long age in the deep delved earth,
Tasting of flora and the country green,
Dance and provençal song and sunburnt mirth.

JOHN KEATS

Acknowledgments

The author wishes to thank the following
people and establishments for their
contributions, inspiration, and support.

Yvonne Gleeson, research assistance
Bob and Ferne Gleeson
Richard and Isabel Gomes
Carey Charlesworth
The Ballard Inn, Santa Ynez Valley
Temecula Creek Inn, Temecula
The Inn, Rancho Santa Fe

Contents

Introduction

Close your eyes for a moment and picture the California wine country. Do you imagine it from aboard a gondola at Sterling Vineyards near Calistoga? Maybe you see the famous stone cellars of the Christian Brothers in St. Helena. Or does the fairytale façade of Rutherford's Inglenook Winery come to mind? Not too many of us conjure images of the breezy, open-air tasting room of Sanford Winery in Buellton; the gleaming pink walls of the château-style Brander winery in Los Olivos; or the century-old stone fireplace that warms winter visitors at York Mountain Winery near Templeton.

For as long as most of us can remember, the cool climes of Northern California have been thought of as exclusively well suited to grapes as motion pictures are to the sunny south. But all that's changing. Within the past few years, the diverse regions of Southern California—from San Diego to Soledad—have begun to command attention throughout the wine world.

It's not that wine is completely new to the southland. Grapes have been grown here since Spanish priests established the missions a couple of centuries ago and began making sacramental wine. In later years, much of the region's bountiful grape harvest was typically sent north for processing into anonymous bulk wines. In the past few years, however, dedicated Southern California winemakers have aptly demonstrated that quality, award-winning wines can be produced exclusively from grapes grown in their own backyards.

For example, wineries of the Paso Robles area are creating some of the state's best Zinfandels and Merlots. The San Luis Obispo area, one of the state's newest wine regions, is blessed with a mild climate that winemakers are fast discovering is well suited to a full range of wines, from Chardonnay to Cabernet. Farther south, the winemakers of the Santa Barbara area are being credited with top-flight Pinot Noirs, as well as other varietals.

NOT A CRITIC'S GUIDE

Our criteria for selecting Southern California wineries were simple. We skipped over every winery and tasting room along bustling Highway 101 and Interstate 5. And we weren't necessarily guided by wine critics or numbers of county fair awards won. In fact, we passed over a few small establishments whose wines are trumpeted far and wide. Why? This being primarily a tour guide, we were more impressed by people and places than ribbons and reviews. Sure, a particular small country winery might concoct a magnificent wine. But if it's produced and poured in an anonymous cinder-block warehouse, we'd rather order a case by mail and spend our Saturday visiting wineries with character and charm. With this strategy we were delighted to discover on many a foray a great new wine (or two) that the critics hadn't heard of.

Although most of the rural Southern California wineries we visited are every bit as charming as those to the north, they remain relatively undiscovered. Unlike the wine roads of the north state, which at times resemble a Southern California freeway, the back roads of the southland aren't plagued by traffic snarls or crowded tasting bars. Very often, the tasting rooms and the hosts were ours alone to enjoy.

WINE RECOMMENDATIONS

While visiting the small wineries featured in this guide, we discovered many wonderful vintages. Unfortunately, by the time the book went to press, most of the wares we sampled had been sold. (One winery we're familiar with produced only twenty-eight cases of a particular vintage.) While some wines improve with age, books that describe them don't. Because of their long shelf life, books simply are not very useful as consumer guides to specific vintages. (Vintage refers to the year during which the grapes were harvested and fermented.)

Consequently, enthusiastic endorsements and flowery descriptions of specific vintages aren't a part of this guide. We don't believe it serves any purpose to carry on about Peachy Canyon Winery's 1990 Westside Zinfandel when you can't buy a bottle.

VINTNERS' CHOICES

Not wanting to send you blindly onto the back roads, we've asked the winemakers at each establishment to name a red and a white of which they are consistently proud. While these "vintner's choice" wines might be subject to change from year to year, depending on the conditions, you can glean from them where a particular winery's strengths lie. Also included are observations about certain wines we enjoyed.

If you're interested in the current year's recommendations, pick up a copy of a wine or food magazine. Reviews of vintages from our backroad wineries are often included. In addition, many of the wineries described in these pages publish regular newsletters that share information about new releases with customers. These are free and may be requested by phone or by writing or at the time of your visit.

Better yet, jump in the car and make your own discoveries. If you wait to read about them in newspapers or magazines, you might be too late. On California's back roads, the early bird gets the best wine.

MAKING AN APPOINTMENT
Making an appointment to taste wine may sound somewhat off-putting, but owners of small wineries don't request it out of arrogance. These folks spend a good part of their day tending wines and vines. If you drop by unannounced, you may find your hosts in the lab, pruning vines, irrigating fields, or otherwise occupied. For most vintners who request a call in advance, twenty-four hours notice is generally sufficient.

RESPONSIBLE TOURING
Backroad wine touring can be one of the most pleasant ways to spend a day or a weekend. Don't spoil your day (or someone else's) by over-indulging at the tasting bar or picnic table. According to California Highway Patrol guide-lines, drinking more than eight ounces of wine over a two-hour period could put you into the "driving under the influence" category. Remember, those little wine samples add up quickly.

We suggest you designate a nondrinking driver for your winery tour and reward him or her with a bottle or two to enjoy later. Many wineries serve complimentary coffee, soda, or grape juice to designated drivers. Please do your part to keep the back-country wine roads safe.

A FINAL NOTE
No payment was sought or accepted from any establishment in exchange for being featured in this book.

A FOOTNOTE: PHYLLOXERA
We didn't feel that our newly revised guide to small California wineries would be complete without some mention of a development that is having a great impact on many of the state's vineyards during this decade.

No doubt by now most California wine enthusiasts have read about or witnessed the destructive effects on our vineyards of the phylloxera louse. This particularly virulent mutant strain of phylloxera, first spotted in Napa Valley in 1979, is now systematically working its way through the state—even into Southern California. These prolific parasites can't be stopped by pesticides and the bugs ultimately kill the vines they attack.

Vineyard owners whose vines have become infested with phylloxera have no choice but to replant with rootstock that is more resistant. You'll see many spindly, young vines during your backroad winery tours as growers do battle with the destructive louse.

It's estimated that the infestation will cost grape growers and winemakers a half-billion dollars over the next decade or two. Expect at least part of the cost to be passed along to consumers in the form of higher wine prices, especially in the regions hardest hit by phylloxera.

Before Your Tour

Even though the winemaker or owner might be the one pouring samples at a backroad winery, don't be embarrassed if you're new to the wine-tasting game. Winemakers as well as tasting-bar hosts have their own special methods for tasting, and they're happy to pass along their techniques to visitors. You will generally start with dry white wines, moving next to sweet whites, and finishing with reds.

How to Taste Wine

See

Hold your glass at eye level and take note of the wine's color and clarity. The wine shouldn't appear cloudy or dull (sediment is okay). Red wines become lighter as they age while white wines darken as they get older.

Swirl

Gently swirl the glass, releasing the wine's aroma and bouquet. (*Aroma* is the smell of the grape in the wine; *bouquet* refers to the scents that result from aging and fermentation.)

Sniff

Bring the glass close to your nose and inhale deeply. Try to pick out the different scents. Smelling a wine is important since most of what you think is taste is in fact linked to smell. Most of the time you'll be greeted by pleasant aromas, but olfactory warning signs include a burning match smell (too much sulfur dioxide preservative) or a sour smell (too much acetic acid).

Sip

Take a sip of the wine and swirl it around in your mouth, making sure it encounters your whole tongue, so you'll be able to pick up all the subtle tastes. You'll notice definite flavors and sensations. Try to describe the wine's *body*, or mouthfeel. Is it light, medium, or full bodied?

Savor

After you swallow, take a moment to savor the lingering tastes and sensations in your mouth. This impression is referred to as the wine's *finish*.

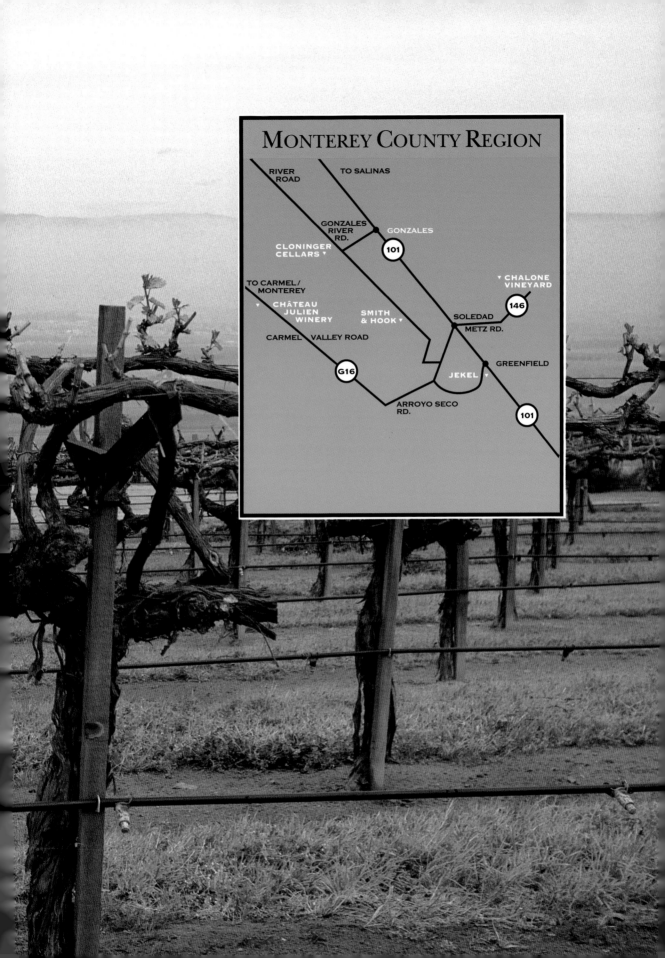

MONTEREY COUNTY REGION

RIVER ROAD

TO SALINAS

GONZALES RIVER RD.

GONZALES

101

CLONINGER CELLARS ▾

▾ CHALONE VINEYARD

TO CARMEL/ MONTEREY

146

▾ CHÂTEAU JULIEN WINERY

SMITH & HOOK ▾

SOLEDAD

METZ RD.

CARMEL VALLEY ROAD

G16

JEKEL ▾

GREENFIELD

ARROYO SECO RD.

101

CLONINGER CELLARS TASTING ROOM

Gonzales

In the early 1980s, Loren Cloninger combined his career in farming with a home winemaking hobby. Over a period of about eight years, Loren's home vintages became so well regarded that his friends convinced him to sell his Chardonnay and Cabernet Sauvignon commercially. Loren, whose family has been farming in the Monterey County area for three generations, teamed with the owners of Boskovich Farms and two other families to officially christen the Cloninger Cellars label in 1988.

Cloninger cultivates an expanding vineyard on Selva Ranch, located within the prime River Road growing area above Gonzales. Plans are to expand the vineyard ultimately to two-hundred acres. A winemaking facility on the vineyard site is also part of the long-range plan.

A new outlet for Cloninger wines was created in 1993 when the partners converted an old Cloninger family dairy farm into a tasting room. Visitors have access to a picnic area with views to the Salinas River, and tours of the nearby vineyard may be arranged by appointment.

Until a dedicated winery is built, Cloninger's winemaker/partner, John Estell, uses the facilities at Paul Masson Winery in Soledad to barrel-ferment, age, and bottle. About five-thousand cases are produced each year.

THE WINE LIST
Chardonnay
Cabernet Sauvignon
Pinot Noir

VINTNER'S CHOICES
WHITE: *Chardonnay*
RED: *Pinot Noir*

CLONINGER CELLARS
TASTING ROOM
1645 RIVER ROAD
GONZALES, CA 93926
(408) 758-1686

HOURS: *10:30 a.m.-6 p.m. Thursday through Monday*

TASTINGS: *Yes*
CHARGE FOR TASTING: *No*
TOURS: *Vineyard tours available by appointment*
PICNIC AREA: *Yes*
RETAIL SALES: *Yes*

DIRECTIONS: *From northbound Highway 101, take Gonzales exit and drive into town. Turn left on River Road and drive two miles to winery on right. From southbound Highway 101 in Salinas, drive south on Highway 68. Exit at River Road and drive south sixteen miles to winery on left.*

JEKEL VINEYARD

Greenfield

From a distance, the grounds of Jekel Vineyard more closely resemble a rambling country estate. In addition to a weathered old barn, there's a windmill and long, two-story building that from the road resembles a fine old ranch house. A winery it is, however, albeit a new one. The Jekel family planted their first vines in 1972 on the site of a former dairy farm at the edge of town. The winery followed six years later.

Well-suited to grapes, Jekel Vineyard is planted in coarse, gravelly soil deposited by the Arroyo Seco River that wound through this area

long ago. The rocky soil provides optimal drainage for the more than three-hundred acres of vines. The vineyard supplies enough grapes to drive Jekel's annual production of fifty-thousand cases.

Among the wines is an award-winning Cabernet Sauvignon, which caught the attention of the Joint Congressional Committee on Inaugural Ceremonies. The committee chose Jekel's

1989 Estate-Bottled Arroyo Seco Cabernet Sauvignon to pour at President Clinton's inaugural luncheon in the U.S. Capitol in 1993. Also noteworthy are Jekel's two proprietary wines. Jekel Sceptre is an exclusive Chardonnay whose grapes come from a single vineyard, while Jekel Symmetry is a blend of Cabernet Sauvignon, Merlot, and Cabernet Franc.

Although the Jekel family is still very much involved, the business is now owned by the Brown-Forman Beverage Corporation. Brown-Forman also operates Korbel Champagne Cellars and Fetzer Winery.

Production at Jekel is centered in a large metal barn painted red. Towering stainless steel fermenters, a laboratory, barrel storage, and a bottling room are within a few steps of each other. While a tour of Jekel's facilities is worthwhile, visitors can also view some of the operation from interior windows in the small tasting room and retail shop.

THE WINE LIST
Chardonnay
Jekel Sceptre Chardonnay
Johannisberg Riesling
Late Harvest Riesling
Cabernet Franc
Cabernet Sauvignon
Jekel Symmetry Meritage
Merlot
Pinot Noir

VINTNER'S CHOICES
WHITE: *Chardonnay*
RED: *Cabernet Franc*

JEKEL VINEYARD
40155 WALNUT AVENUE
GREENFIELD, CA 93927
(408) 674-5522

HOURS: *10 a.m.-5 p.m. daily*
TASTINGS: *Yes*
CHARGE FOR TASTING: *No*
TOURS: *By appointment*
PICNIC AREA: *Yes*
RETAIL SALES: *Yes*

DIRECTIONS: *From Highway 101, take the Walnut Avenue exit and drive west approximately one mile to winery on right.*

SMITH & HOOK

Soledad

Smith & Hook is proof that the best wineries are usually the ones at the end of the longest, dustiest roads. The back road to Smith & Hook took us about half way up the beautiful Santa Lucia Highlands on the west side of the Salinas Valley. It's in the unusual microclimate here that some of the state's most consistently high quality red wines are created.

Much of the operation is housed in an old barn whose former occupants were quarter horses; the site was formerly a horse ranch. The converted stable sits on the old Smith Ranch, while the adjacent Hook property, once a cattle ranch, contains the original Cabernet

Sauvignon vineyard—hence the winery's name.

The site, which affords breathtaking views across the valley to the Gavilan Range, was chosen in the mid-1970s by the McFarland Wine Company of Southern California. The McFarlands, longtime wine grape growers, concentrated their initial planting efforts on Cabernet vines.

The winery was purchased in 1981 by Swiss native Nicholaus Hahn, who at one time was the youngest vice president of Rothschild Bank in Zurich. He later became chairman of one of the world's largest independent computer software companies. During his tenure at the helm of Smith & Hook, Nicholaus has expanded the operation considerably. With over two-hundred-fifty acres now spread among

five vineyards, the winery is said to be one of the nation's largest growers of Merlot and Cabernet Franc.

Although the function of the old Smith horse ranch has been dramatically altered, the proprietors have preserved the property's rustic look. The stable, whose Dutch-style horse doors are still in place, was reconditioned to house winemaking equipment, redwood fermenting tanks, and rows of barrels. The old tack room is now the laboratory, and what was a bunkhouse for the wranglers now serves as an office.

Tastings take place nearby inside a twenty-eight-thousand-gallon redwood tank that was once used for aging wines. Here you'll find wines bottled under both the Smith & Hook label and the Hahn Estates label.

THE WINE LIST
Chardonnay
Cabernet Franc
Cabernet Sauvignon
Merlot

VINTNER'S CHOICES
WHITE: *Hahn Estates Chardonnay*
RED: *Smith & Hook Cabernet
    Sauvignon*

SMITH & HOOK
37700 FOOTHILL ROAD
GONZALES, CA 93926
(408) 678-2132

HOURS: *11 a.m.-4 p.m. daily*
TASTINGS: *Yes*
CHARGE FOR TASTING: *No*
TOURS: *On request*
PICNIC AREA: *Yes*
RETAIL SALES: *Yes*

DIRECTIONS: *From Highway 101, exit west on Arroyo Seco Road, and turn right on Fort Romie Road. Turn left on Colony Road and right on Foothill Road. Turn left at the winery sign and drive to winery at the end of the road.*

CHALONE VINEYARD

Soledad

*O*ur most recent trip to Chalone Vineyard came on the heels of a series of storms that turned the hills of the Gavilan range a lusciously deep green. Every twist and turn in the narrow road revealed ethereal scenes of velvety valleys and majestic oaks shimmering in the sun with new foliage. Finally, the Pinnacles National Monument came into view, crowning the carpeted hilltops with a spectacular display of craggy peaks.

Situated a stone's throw from the jagged outcroppings, Chalone derives its name from the Ohlone Indians who populated this part of the Gavilan range area long ago. Although grapes have been grown on the Chalone site since the early 1900s, it wasn't until Harvard-trained musician Richard Graff came on the scene in the 1960s that greater numbers of premium vines were coaxed from the dry, rocky soil. Because the region receives only a dozen or so inches of rain

during a wet year, Dick was among the early handful of farmers to experiment with drip irrigation. His success is evident; the vineyards of Pinot Blanc, Chardonnay, Pinot Noir, and Chenin Blanc grapes comprise an impressive 160 acres.

In addition to expanding the vineyard, Dick has brought the business a long way since he made wine here in a converted chicken coop some three decades ago. He now serves as chairman and chief operating officer of Chalone Incorporated, one of few publicly held wine companies in the United States. The company also operates Edna Valley Vineyard in San Luis Obispo (see separate listing in this book) and Acacia Winery in Napa, and is a partner in Caramenet Vineyard in Sonoma.

Today, Chalone's tidy little original winery is dwarfed by a large, contemporary building carved into a hillside. The tasting room, reached by an outdoor staircase from the parking area, has a balcony that commands a stunning view of the vineyards and hills beyond. Visitors who make the twenty-minute trek from the valley floor are treated to a comprehensive one-and-a-half-hour tour that encompasses every aspect of Chalone's winemaking process. You'll even get a chance to descend into the cool caves where Chalone wines go to age.

By the way, Chalone stock is publicly traded over the counter and is quoted on the NASDAQ National Market System under the symbol CHLN. Those holding one-hundred shares or more are treated to "special benefits" including an annual stockholder's gala.

THE WINE LIST
Chardonnay
Chenin Blanc
Pinot Blanc
Pinot Noir

VINTNER'S CHOICES
WHITE: *Chardonnay*
RED: *Pinot Noir*

CHALONE VINEYARD
P.O. BOX 855
SOLEDAD, CA 93960
(408) 678-1717

HOURS: *Weekdays by appointment; 11:30 a.m.-4 p.m. Saturday and Sunday*
TASTINGS: *Yes*
CHARGE FOR TASTING: *No*
TOURS: *Appointment needed for weekday tours; none needed during weekend hours*
PICNIC AREA: *Yes*
RETAIL SALES: *Yes*

DIRECTIONS: *From Soledad, drive east on Metz Road for two-and-a-half miles. Turn left with Highway 146 and follow for another five-and-a-half miles. Turn left onto the dirt road at the Chalone sign and follow to winery, bearing right when a choice presents itself.*

CHÂTEAU JULIEN

Carmel

The corporate offices of an East Coast oil company are a long way, both physically and figuratively, from a wine estate on the California coast. Nonetheless, petroleum company executive Bob Brower and his wife, Pat, were happy to trade their existence in New York for life in peaceful Carmel.

As the winery's name and appearance suggest, the Browers were inspired by the fine country wineries of France. Wines are produced in the French claret tradition of Bordeaux, using contemporary

equipment and imported bottles. The French oak cooperage is exchanged for new barrels after each vintage.

The winery, which has become a landmark of sorts along Carmel Valley Road, is an impressive two-story building of white plaster. Built in

1983, it contains a private dining room and outdoor garden for private gatherings. Tastings take place in the Great Hall under a soaring cathedral ceiling. Stroll onto the back patio and you'll see the production equipment just off to the side.

Château Julien has only a small experimental vineyard on site and consequently purchases grapes from growers elsewhere in Monterey County. In addition to making a select few wines that carry the Château Julien label, the winery bottles more than a half-dozen varieties under the names Garland Ranch and Emerald Bay.

THE WINE LIST
Chardonnay
Gewürztraminer
Johannisberg Riesling
Sauvignon Blanc
White table wine
Cabernet Sauvignon
Merlot
Napa Gamay

VINTNER'S CHOICES
WHITE: *Chardonnay*
RED: *Merlot*

CHÂTEAU JULIEN
8940 CARMEL VALLEY ROAD
CARMEL, CA 93923
(408) 624-2600

HOURS: *8:30 a.m.-5 p.m. weekdays;*
11 a.m.-5 p.m. weekends
TASTINGS: *Yes*
CHARGE FOR TASTING: *No*
TOURS: *By appointment*
PICNIC AREA: *Yes*
RETAIL SALES: *Yes*

DIRECTIONS: *From Carmel,*
drive east for five miles on
G-16/Carmel Valley Road to
winery on right.

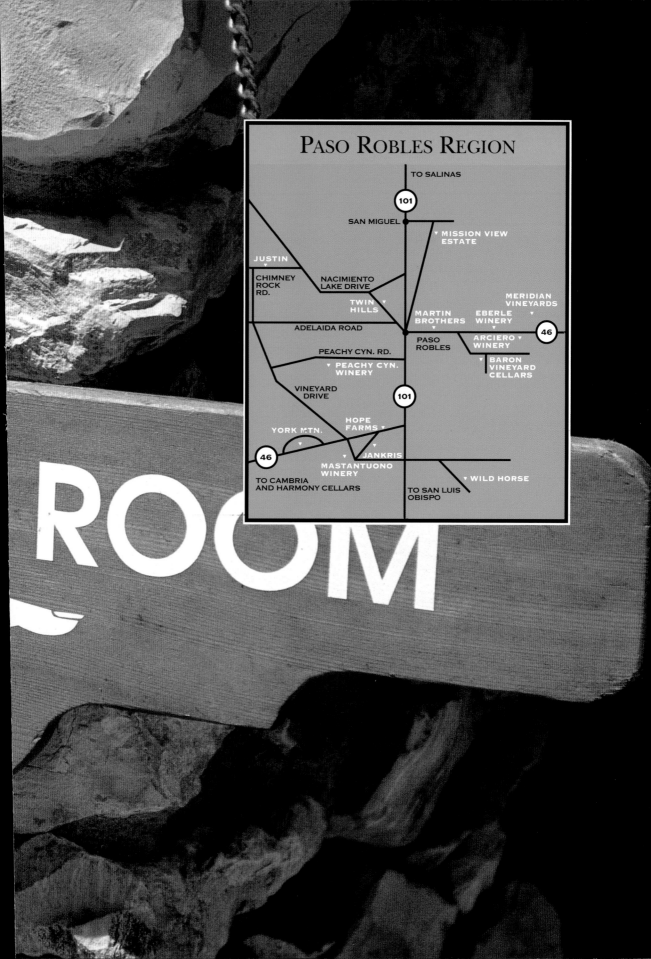

PASO ROBLES REGION

TO SALINAS

101

SAN MIGUEL

▼ MISSION VIEW
ESTATE

JUSTIN
▼

CHIMNEY
ROCK
RD.

NACIMIENTO
LAKE DRIVE

MERIDIAN
VINEYARDS
▼

TWIN
HILLS ▼

MARTIN
BROTHERS
▼

EBERLE
WINERY
▼

ADELAIDA ROAD

PASO
ROBLES

ARCIERO ▼
WINERY

46

PEACHY CYN. RD.

▼ PEACHY CYN.
WINERY

▼ BARON
VINEYARD
CELLARS

VINEYARD
DRIVE

101

YORK MTN.
▼

HOPE
FARMS ▼

46

▼

JANKRIS

MASTANTUONO
WINERY

TO CAMBRIA
AND HARMONY CELLARS

TO SAN LUIS
OBISPO

▼ WILD HORSE

MISSION VIEW ESTATE

San Miguel

Cathy and Terry Peterson stretched the northern boundary of the Paso Robles area wine country a few years ago when they established a new vineyard and winery in the golden hills overlooking the hamlet of San Miguel. Mission View Estate is far removed from the main Paso Robles winery clusters, but it occupies a spot that has turned out to be well suited to growing grapes. The fifty acres of vines are planted in gravel and loam alluvial soils that produce high-quality fruit but in low yields. Combine these soil conditions with wide temperature swings and you've got the primary essentials for some special wines.

Now owned by an investment group, Mission View Estate has continued the tradition of handcrafting wines with an emphasis on quality rather than quantity. Only around five-thousand cases are produced each year, and the winery restricts sales of its limited releases to six bottles per customer.

Open for tours by appointment, the winery is housed in a two-level barn-style building overlooking the vineyards. Across the parking area is a storage facility topped by what used to be a tasting room. This facility is now used for many special events held throughout the year.

Although the winery is a few miles off the beaten path, the owners have made their wines more accessible through the operation of a tasting room just south of Mission San Miguel Arcangel, at the Wellsona Road exit from Highway 101.

THE WINE LIST
Chardonnay
Muscat Canelli
Sauvignon Blanc
Cabernet Sauvignon
Pinot Noir
Zinfandel

VINTNER'S CHOICES
WHITE: *Sauvignon Blanc*
RED: *Cabernet Sauvignon*

MISSION VIEW ESTATE
WINERY ADDRESS:
13350 NORTH RIVER ROAD
SAN MIGUEL, CA 93451
TASTING ROOM LOCATION:
HIGHWAY 101 AT
WELLSONA ROAD
(805) 467-3104

HOURS: *Tasting room: Winter hours, 10 a.m.-5 p.m. daily; summer hours, 10 a.m.-6 p.m. daily*
TASTINGS: *Yes*
CHARGE FOR TASTING: *For library reserve and limited release selections*
TOURS: *Of winery only by appointment*
PICNIC AREA: *At winery (by appointment) and tasting room*
RETAIL SALES: *Yes*

DIRECTIONS: *The tasting room is located between Paso Robles and San Miguel on the east side of Highway 101 at the Wellsona Road exit. Call for winery tour appointment and directions.*

TWIN HILLS WINERY

Paso Robles

*N*ary another soul ventured into the attractive tasting room of *Twin Hills Winery during our visit on a beautiful spring afternoon. As evidenced by the steady stream of boat-towing vehicles passing by on the way to Lake Nacimiento, most of the locals were more interested in water sports than a relaxing visit to one of the region's most cozy tasting rooms.*

The newest owners of Twin Hills—Glenn Reid and Caroline Scott— trace their winemaking roots to Caroline's college days at Stanford University in the early 1980s. During a break from her chemical engineering studies, Caroline, along with a college buddy, created a batch of Zinfandel in a garage. After that vintage, home winemaking quickly became Caroline's avocational passion. A few years later she married Glenn, who was also bitten by the winemaking bug. Together they realized a dream in 1992 by buying Twin Hills.

The tasting room, which sits next to busy Lake Nacimiento Drive just outside Paso Robles, is decorated with French country flair and is furnished with comfy couches placed in front of a large fireplace. Works by local artists are often on display, as is a large selection of gift items. Outside is a lattice-shaded picnic area.

The tasting room is only a small part of the Twin Hills operation. Some forty acres of vineyards and a large production facility are hidden away among the hills across the road. Annual production is approximately five-thousand cases. Among the notable products concocted by Twin Hills is a California Dry Sherry made from Palomino grapes using the old Spanish technique of natural fermentation instead of the typical California method of artificial baking.

In addition to running a winery, Caroline and Glenn operate Fluid Control Systems, a consulting firm that works with businesses to protect the public and environment from hazardous chemicals and materials. The couple practices what they preach. Herbicides are not used in the Twin Hills vineyards. Instead they control the weeds the old-fashioned way with a French hoe.

THE WINE LIST
Chardonnay
Johannisberg Riesling
White Zinfandel
Cabernet Sauvignon
California Beaujolais
Port
Sherry
Zinfandel
Zinfandel Rosé

VINTNER'S CHOICES
WHITE: *Chardonnay*
RED: *Zinfandel*

TWIN HILLS WINERY
2025 LAKE NACIMIENTO DRIVE
PASO ROBLES, CA 93446
(805) 238-9148

HOURS: *Winter hours, 12 Noon-4 p.m. daily; summer hours, 11 a.m.-5 p.m. daily*
TASTINGS: *Yes*
CHARGE FOR TASTING: *No*
TOURS: *By appointment*
PICNIC AREA: *Yes*
RETAIL SALES: *Yes*

DIRECTIONS: *From Highway 101, exit at Lake Nacimiento/ Highway 46 (24th Street) and drive west through town toward Lake Nacimiento. Winery is on the right approximately four miles out of town.*

JUSTIN VINEYARDS AND WINERY

Paso Robles

We had no map when we set out into the Santa Lucia foothills looking for Justin Vineyards and Winery; we were armed only with a suggestion from a local vintner that the winery on Chimney Rock Road was worth a visit. Five miles out of Paso Robles, after countless twists and turns along a deserted country road, I was skeptical; at the six mile point I was ready to turn around. "Let's give it one more mile," my companion suggested. Grudgingly, I stayed the course, and just as mile seven loomed on the odometer, so did the stone wall of what we concluded was the most enchanting winemaking operation in the Paso Robles region.

The winery's namesake is Justin Baldwin, who along with his wife, Deborah, established this veritable wine oasis in the middle of nowhere in 1987. In making the decision to create a winery, Justin and Deborah, both former bankers from the Los Angeles area, opted against becoming another "pretty face" along the well-traveled wine roads of Napa and Sonoma valleys. Instead they chose this remote part of the Adelaida Valley that had previously been used to dry-farm barley for cattle feeding.

Justin started with a seventy-two-acre vineyard in 1982, encircling it with two miles of electrified fencing to discourage the local deer, boar, and wild turkeys who love grapes as much as we do. After the winery was built in the late 1980s, construction began on a French auberge-style tasting room and visitor center. The striking compound, which also includes the Baldwin residence, is accented by fieldstone trimmings, metal roofs, multipaned windows, and vivid yellow canopies. A mature English flower and herb garden is icing on the cake.

Among the more noteworthy wines produced here is Isosceles Reserve, a Meritage blend of Cabernet Sauvignon, Merlot, and Cabernet Franc. One of only a few one-hundred-percent estate Meritage wines made in the nation, Isosceles Reserve ages for a whopping thirty-two months in small French oak barrels before blending.

In addition to producing wine, the Baldwins make and market what they describe as the world's first one-hundred-percent estate vintage Cabernet Sauvignon sorbet.

Finally, the couple also operates the Just Inn. The small bed-and-breakfast operation consists of two lavishly decadent suites that sit above the winery. Both are equipped with fireplaces and tubs big enough for two. Reserve these early; they're booked far in advance for romantic weekend sleepovers.

THE WINE LIST
Chardonnay
Cabernet Franc
Cabernet Sauvignon
Isosceles Reserve Meritage
Merlot
Nebbiolo

VINTNER'S CHOICES
WHITE: *Chardonnay*
RED: *Isosceles Reserve Meritage*

JUSTIN VINEYARDS AND WINERY
11680 CHIMNEY ROCK ROAD
PASO ROBLES, CA 93446
(805) 238-6932

HOURS: *9 a.m.-5 p.m. daily*
TASTINGS: *Yes*
CHARGE FOR TASTING: *No*
TOURS: *Yes*
PICNIC AREA: *Yes*
RETAIL SALES: *Yes*

DIRECTIONS: *From the intersection of Highways 46 east and 101, drive eight miles west initially on Twenty-fourth Street which becomes Lake Nacimiento Road. Continue to Chimney Rock Road and drive west on Chimney Rock Road another seven miles to winery on right.*

PEACHY CANYON WINERY

Paso Robles

*S*ure, we were welcome to drive out to the winery, proprietor Doug *Beckett told us over the phone one spring morning. "But you should know," he said. "I don't have any wine left."*

Such is the predicament of a vintner who produces small amounts of coveted wines. Peachy Canyon's three-thousand cases of Zinfandel, Cabernet Sauvignon, and Merlot typically are snatched up by eager retailers and distributors within several days of their release each year.

From his second-floor office atop a modest winery, Doug explained his lack of inventory to multiple callers while describing a "Walter Mitty life." His first career was as a teacher, during which he pursued an avocation of buying and selling autographs of famous people. Doug's office was decorated with numerous acquisitions, including an original animation cell from Fantasia along with the signature of its late creator, Walt Disney. The scrawl of Babe Ruth and original notes from the hand of Buffalo Bill Cody were also displayed.

Following his teaching stint, Doug built a Southern California chain of liquor stores and restaurants, did some land developing, and dabbled in home winemaking. Later he became a partner in tiny Tobias Winery, an operation known during the 1980s for Petite Sirah and Zinfandel.

After scouting the area for a site for his own winery, Doug settled on a thirty-acre hilltop crowned with a reproduction New England farmhouse whose image graces the Peachy Canyon label. The winery, built in 1988, sits behind the house, surrounded by approximately a half-dozen acres of young vines growing on sloping land.

Peachy Canyon's consistently highly rated product line includes no white wines, reflecting Doug's passion for hearty reds. Rather than spread his talents among several wines, Doug prefers to be a "master of one or two good wines."

So how does one go about securing a rare bottle of Peachy Canyon wine? The best bet is to attend one of the little winery's two open houses held each year. For these events, held after the local Paderewski Festival and the Paso Robles Wine Festival, Doug holds back several cases to offer for sale to visitors. For information about the open houses, write to the winery.

THE WINE LIST
Cabernet Sauvignon
Merlot
Zinfandel

VINTNER'S CHOICES
RED: *Zinfandel*

PEACHY CANYON WINERY
ROUTE 1, BOX 115C
PASO ROBLES, CA 93446
(805) 237-1577

HOURS: *By appointment*
TASTINGS: *By appointment, if wine is available*
CHARGE FOR TASTING: *No*
TOURS: *By appointment*
PICNIC AREA: *No*
RETAIL SALES: *If wine is available*

DIRECTIONS: *From Highway 101 in Paso Robles, exit at Spring Street. Drive west on Sixth Street, turn right on Olive Drive, then make an immediate left onto Peachy Canyon Drive. Drive six miles to winery on left.*

HOPE FARMS WINERY

Paso Robles

*A*lthough backroad winemaking is very much an agricultural *pursuit, we meet few boutique vintners who actually had farming experience before they began crushing grapes. There are plenty of former teachers, engineers, and lawyers making wine these days, but few former farmers.*

Brothers Chuck and Paul Hope, rarities in the winemaking industry, farmed for more than a decade before opening their namesake winery in 1989. Moving from the Central Valley in 1978, Chuck and Paul, along with their wives, Marlyn and Janet, settled on land near San Miguel and began growing grapes and apples. After several years of selling their grape crop to other vintners, the siblings decided to hold the best fruit from their more than two-hundred acres of vines and create wines. Only about ten percent of the annual harvest is set aside for Hope Farms wines.

The family-run operation specializes in red wines that according to winemaker Steve Rasmussen are "easy drinking; not big tannic monsters, but wines that are accessible, readily drinkable, and able to age."

Samples of the family's half-dozen or so varieties are poured at a picturesque facility along Highway 46 west of Paso Robles. If it weren't for the sign out front, passersby might at first glance mistake the compound for an elegant Victorian estate. Guests are welcomed at a sparkling white farmhouse with a wraparound porch. A matching gazebo sits on the front lawn. In addition to wine, the oak-trimmed tasting room sells numerous gourmet goodies and delicatessen items.

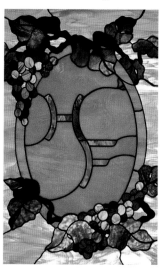

THE WINE LIST
Chardonnay
Muscat Canelli
White Zinfandel
Cabernet Sauvignon
Claret
Zinfandel

VINTNER'S CHOICES
WHITE: *Chardonnay*
RED: *Cabernet Sauvignon*

HOPE FARMS
2175 ARBOR ROAD
PASO ROBLES, CA 93447
(805) 238-6979

HOURS: *11 a.m.-5 p.m. daily*
TASTINGS: *Yes*
CHARGE FOR TASTING: *Yes*
TOURS: *No*
PICNIC AREA: *Yes*
RETAIL SALES: *Yes*

DIRECTIONS: *From Highway 101 in Paso Robles, exit at westbound Highway 46 and drive to winery on the right at Arbor Road.*

JANKRIS WINERY

Templeton

*W*hen Mark and Paula Gendron chose an identity for their new winery in 1991, they could have done what most backroad vintners do. They could easily have christened it after themselves or their street, or derived a name from the beautiful oak-studded terrain on which their vineyards grow. Instead, Mark and Paula combined the names of their two young daughters, commissioning a cute label featuring the girls' silhouettes. Unfortunately, January and Kristin

won't be of legal age to taste their namesake beverages for several more years. The siblings were still in grade school when their mom and dad created the winery.

Although their participation in the winery is limited by school and homework, Jan and Kris are quite active on the ranch. In the fall you might see them in the vineyards with the crews, scouting the best grapes and helping to hand-pick the harvest. Springtime often finds them feeding the horses and other critters who share the property.

The barn and friendly animals are attention getters, but the ranch's centerpiece is a century-old Victorian farmhouse. Set under a sprawling old oak tree, the two-story structure now houses the tasting room and winery offices. Out front near the road is a freestanding glass-enclosed gazebo, which is rented for special events.

The surrounding forty-plus-acre vineyard provides much of the fruit for JanKris's annual production of two-thousand-five-hundred cases. Included in the wine list is a gold medal–winning Merlot.

THE WINE LIST
Chardonnay
White Zinfandel
Gamay
Merlot
Pinot Noir
Zinfandel

VINTNER'S CHOICES
WHITE: *Chardonnay*
RED: *Merlot*

JANKRIS WINERY
ROUTE 2, BOX 40-B, BETHEL ROAD
TEMPLETON, CA 93465
(805) 434-0319

HOURS: *11 a.m.-5:30 p.m. daily*
TASTINGS: *Yes*
CHARGE FOR TASTING: *Yes*
TOURS: *No*
PICNIC AREA: *Yes*
RETAIL SALES: *Yes*

DIRECTIONS: *From Highway 101 in Paso Robles, exit at westbound Highway 46 and drive to Bethel Road. Turn left on Bethel and drive approximately five-hundred feet to winery on left.*

MASTANTUONO WINERY

Templeton

From the road, the French château-style façade of Mastantuono Winery makes a rather formal statement. But don't be fooled. Visitors expecting hushed voices, classical music, and chandeliers will be in for a pleasant surprise. Staid and stodgy it isn't.

Pasquale Mastantuono, aka Pat Mastan or the Zin Man, imbued his tasting room with the same zest and energy that characterizes his colorful personality. The swordfish and wild boar trophies on the wall tell of his fondness for fishing and hunting, while a passion for history is represented by an antique wine press and collections of old wine-related bric-a-brac. A gleaming 1935 Auburn automobile parked in

the adjacent garage is testament to Pat's success in varied pursuits.

Although Pat didn't cut his teeth in the vineyard, his passion for winemaking preceded by several years the decision to open a winery. Formerly a resident of the Los Angeles area, Pat earlier ran a successful business as a custom furniture designer. Elvis Presley and Sammy Davis, Jr., were among many satisfied customers. In his free time Pat made small amounts of wine.

THE WINE LIST
Aleatico
Champagne
Chardonnay
White Zinfandel
Cabernet Sauvignon
California Port
Carminello
Muscat Canelli
Zinfandel

VINTNER'S CHOICES
WHITE: *Chardonnay*
RED: *Zinfandel*

MASTANTUONO WINERY
100 OAKVIEW ROAD
TEMPLETON, CA 93465
(805) 238-0676

HOURS: *10 a.m.-5 p.m. daily*
TASTINGS: *Yes*
CHARGE FOR TASTING: *No*
TOURS: *No*
PICNIC AREA: *Yes*
RETAIL SALES: *Yes*

DIRECTIONS: *From Highway 101 south of Paso Robles, exit west on Vineyard Drive and drive four miles to winery, on left, near intersection of Vineyard Drive and Highway 46.*

In the early 1980s, the Mastantuono clan moved to the Paso Robles area, where Pat helped launch the region's wine renaissance. Since 1978, when he opened his impressive tasting château a stone's throw from Highway 46, many other winemakers have set up shop nearby.

The winery is probably best known for its rich and robust Zinfandel. After all, they don't call Pat the Zin Man for nothing.

YORK MOUNTAIN WINERY

Templeton

Unlike many of the wineries west of Paso Robles that planted themselves within sight of Highway 46, the patriarch of central coast wineries sits secluded among the oaks off the main road. Relatively undiscovered by the highway crowd on their way to or from the coast, York Mountain Winery is a favorite among locals in the know, despite its lack of glitz and glamour.

Like a good wine, the place appears to have improved with age. Built in 1882, the winery is still brimming with charm and character,

from the hand-formed brick façade to the rustic, eclectic interior with its huge field-stone fireplace and dark wooden floors. It's Southern California's quintessential backroad winery.

Although the winery is over a century old, it has changed family hands but once. Andrew York established the business as Ascension Winery, passing it along to two later generations of Yorks. The family finally sold the winery in 1970 to wine and spirits industry executive Max Goldman.

Following the tradition set by Andrew York, Max has involved his own children in the business. These days the winery is primarily in the hands of Max's son Steve, who serves as winemaker and manager, and daughter Suzanne, who manages the tasting room.

The vintage tasting room, voted by readers of a local newspaper as the best in the county, is chockablock with antiques, curios, and gift items. Winter visitors might be greeted by a roaring fire.

In addition to being one of the west's oldest wineries, York Mountain has its own recognized viticultural appellation—one of the smallest in the nation. Available in few stores and restaurants, York Mountain's wines—about five-thousand cases are produced each year—are sold primarily on site to visitors.

THE WINE LIST
Champagne
Chardonnay
White table wine
Cabernet Sauvignon
Merlot
Pinot Noir
Port Dry Sherry
Red table wine
Zinfandel

VINTNER'S CHOICES
WHITE: *Chardonnay*
RED: *Pinot Noir*

YORK MOUNTAIN WINERY
ROUTE 2, BOX 191
TEMPLETON, CA 93465
(805) 238-3925

HOURS: *10 a.m.-5 p.m. daily*
TASTINGS: *Yes*
CHARGE FOR TASTING: *No*
TOURS: *By appointment*
PICNIC AREA: *No*
RETAIL SALES: *Yes*

DIRECTIONS: *From Highway 101 in Paso Robles, exit west on Highway 46 and drive nine miles to York Mountain Road. Turn right on York Mountain Road and drive to winery.*

WILD HORSE WINERY AND VINEYARDS

Templeton

The new tasting room at Wild Horse Winery and Vineyards had been open but a few weeks when we stopped by. Although the two-story French Mediterranean-style winery was built in 1988, Wild Horse staff chose not to open a tasting room right away, focusing their attention instead on developing quality wines. It wasn't until 1993 that the Wild Horse visitors center opened. Even now, visitors are encouraged to make an appointment prior to dropping by. By the way, Wild Horse is among the few area wineries closed during the weekend.

Owner and cellar master Ken Volk established the winery in 1983, choosing a picturesque site on a mesa above the Salinas River. Although the days here are warm, nearby Estero Bay sends cool maritime air over the thirty-five acres of vines.

In 1990, Wild Horse emerged from a list of hundreds as *Wine and Spirits* magazine's winery of the year. The honor was bestowed after

Wild Horse consistently scored the highest point average in blind tastings conducted by the magazine's tasters at the American Wine Competition.

Wild Horse's most notable red wine is Pinot Noir, an award winner whose grapes come from premier vineyards in the Santa Maria area. The winery, which produces about thirty-five-thousand cases of wine each year, has begun experimenting with Semillon, Negrette, and Trousseau, among others.

A graduate of the fruit science program at nearby California Polytechnic State University, Ken is still active with his alma mater, making some wine from grapes grown on campus by Cal Poly students.

THE WINE LIST
Chardonnay
Merlot
Pinot Noir
Cabernet Sauvignon
Zinfandel

VINTNER'S CHOICES
WHITE: *Chardonnay*
RED: *Pinot Noir*

**WILD HORSE WINERY
AND VINEYARDS
2484 TEMPLETON ROAD
TEMPLETON, CA 93465**
(805) 434-2541

HOURS: *8 a.m.-5 p.m. Monday through Friday by appointment*
TASTINGS: *By appointment*
CHARGE FOR TASTING: *No*
TOURS: *By appointment*
PICNIC AREA: *By appointment*
RETAIL SALES: *By appointment*

DIRECTIONS: *At the Templeton exit from Highway 101, drive east on Vineyard Drive over the Salinas River bridge and turn right on Templeton Road. Drive 2.2 miles to Wild Horse Way and turn left (first left turn after Eureka Lane).*

HARMONY CELLARS

Harmony

On the afternoon of our visit to Harmony, we counted two-dozen cows grazing in a pasture along the little town's only street. That's six more cows than people living in this quaint artists' colony that lies about ten miles south of Hearst Castle.

Although a population of eighteen isn't sufficient to support a video rental shop, gas station, or even a grocery store, Harmony does have its own winery—actually, "tasting room" is probably more accurate. At the time we dropped by, owner Kim Mulligan was in the process of building a new winery on Harmony Valley Road, but it

hadn't yet been completed. In the meantime, wines were being poured for visitors in a small tasting room within the old Harmony Valley Creamery Association complex. The old brick building, the largest commercial structure in town, also houses the Harmony Saloon and Harmony Pasta Factory restaurant among several shops. There's also a vintage post office here that's worth a look.

Harmony Cellars winemaker Chuck Mulligan, who holds a degree in enology from California State University, Fresno, handcrafts only about three-thousand-

five-hundred cases per year using grapes purchased from other growers in the region.

Among the products produced by Harmony Cellars is a popular Noel Vineyards Christmas Blush table wine (whose whimsical label depicts two tired elves relaxing with glasses of wine on Christmas Eve) and Zinjolais, a Beaujolais-style Zinfandel.

THE WINE LIST
Chardonnay
Christmas Blush table wine
Johannisberg Riesling
White Zinfandel
Cabernet Sauvignon
Pinot Noir
Zinjolais Zinfandel

VINTNER'S CHOICES
WHITE: *Chardonnay*
RED: *Zinjolais Zinfandel*

HARMONY CELLARS
(TASTING ROOM ONLY)
HARMONY VALLEY ROAD
HARMONY, CA 93435
(805) 239-4295

HOURS: *10 a.m.-5 p.m.*
TASTINGS: *Yes*
CHARGE FOR TASTING: *Yes*
TOURS: *Of winery only by appointment*
PICNIC AREA: *No*
RETAIL SALES: *Yes*

DIRECTIONS: *From Highway One between Cambria and Morro Bay, turn east at the Harmony turnoff and follow Old Creamery Road into town. Tasting room is on the right in the Creamery Association building.*

MARTIN BROTHERS WINERY

Paso Robles

In an industry that all too rarely steps outside traditional bounds, the brothers Martin of Paso Robles are a breath of fresh air. Instead of focusing their attentions exclusively on the tried and true varietals, Tom and Nick Martin hitched their wagon years ago to Nebbiolo, an Italian red wine that is still striving to make a name for itself in California.

The siblings, whose father Edward Martin managed advertising campaigns for Padre Brothers Winery in Cucamonga more than fifty

years ago, began making Nebbiolo in the early 1980s, shortly after the family transformed a Paso Robles dairy farm into a winery and vineyard. Since then, they have continued to finesse and promote this unusual wine, which at three-thousand of the winery's fifteen-thousand cases per year is the brothers' biggest seller.

The Los Angeles Times described a Martin Brothers Nebbiolo as "wonderfully fruity with a sour-cherry aroma and lots of flavor without much of the mouth-puckering tannins that rob a wine of its drinkability." Others have likened Nebbiolo to roasted wood, black currant, and spiced plum fruit.

One plot of Nebbiolo grapes grows adjacent to the winery's modern tasting room and gift shop, which sits just off Highway 46. Connoisseurs of wine label art will have a field day here browsing the Martin Brothers' varied product line. Pencil drawings by da Vinci and Michelangelo are framed in gold foil on the Nebbiolo labels, while the Etrusco Cabernet is emblazoned with a striking gold-embossed lion that rises from a vivid teal-colored background. For the Vin Santo label, the winery chose an extreme close-up, sepia-toned photograph of blades of grass. The Martin Brothers bottling of Aleatico, whose label features a beautiful Botticelli drawing of a mother and child, would be difficult to part with, even after the bottle has been emptied. And those are just for starters. Each wine has its own distinctively attractive label.

In addition to Nick and Tom, the winery calls on the talents of Martin sisters Ann and Mary, sister-in-law Patrice, and brother-in-law David.

THE WINE LIST
Aleatico
Chardonnay
Chenin Blanc
Moscato Allegro
Sauvignon Blanc
Cabernet Sauvignon
Nebbiolo
Zinfandel

VINTNER'S CHOICES
WHITE: *Moscato Allegro*
RED: *Nebbiolo*

MARTIN BROTHERS WINERY
2610 BUENA VISTA DRIVE
PASO ROBLES, CA 93446
(805) 238-2520

HOURS: *11 a.m.-5 p.m. daily*
TASTINGS: *Yes*
CHARGE FOR TASTING: *No*
TOURS: *By appointment*
PICNIC AREA: *Yes*
RETAIL SALES: *Yes*

DIRECTIONS: *From Highway 101 in Paso Robles, exit at Highway 46 and drive east for one-half mile to winery on left.*

BARON VINEYARD CELLARS

Paso Robles

A decade after retirement, former Los Angeles area fire chief Tom Baron has a particularly apparent soft spot in his heart for the profession. Tom's two generic wines, whose labels depict horsedrawn antique firewagons and a fireman trumpeting an alarm, are dedicated to California's firefighters and paramedics. They're appropriately called Firehouse Red and Firehouse White.

For their retirement home, Tom and his wife, Sharon, a former teacher, chose a hilltop a couple of miles off Highway 46 east, near

Paso Robles. However, the couple's retirement was relatively short lived. Tom began growing grapes and in 1987 they opened the Baron Vineyard Cellars.

Don't ask for a tour of the winery. The Barons lease facilities from another winery, so the operation here is strictly tasting and sales. The small cupola-topped tasting room was built next to the Barons' house, providing quick access for Sharon, who serves as the winery's primary visitor hostess. The couple's four daughters also pitch in from time to time, as do their San Francisco Bay Area lawyer son, Bill, and favorite son-in-law, Philippe.

The Baron vineyard consists of just under thirty acres, planted on the hillside below the tasting room. Planted varietals include

Sauvignon Blanc, Muscat Canelli, and Cabernet Sauvignon, which was grafted onto Chenin Blanc rootstock. The soil is chalk-rock, the water is plentiful, and the panoramic view of the Santa Lucia mountain range is impressive.

THE WINE LIST
Chardonnay
Firehouse White table wine
Muscat Canelli
Paso Panache
Sauvignon Blanc
Cabernet Sauvignon
Firehouse Red table wine
Zinfandel

VINTNER'S CHOICES
WHITE: *Sauvignon Blanc*
RED: *Cabernet Sauvignon*

BARON VINEYARD CELLARS
1981 PENMAN SPRINGS ROAD
PASO ROBLES, CA 93446
(805) 239-3313

HOURS: *11 a.m.-5 p.m. Thursday through Monday*
TASTINGS: *Yes*
CHARGE FOR TASTING: *No*
TOURS: *No*
PICNIC AREA: *Yes*
RETAIL SALES: *Yes*

DIRECTIONS: *From Highway 101 in Paso Robles, drive approximately two miles east on Highway 46 and turn south on Union Road. Veer left on Union Road for about two-and-a-half miles to Penman Springs Road. Turn right and follow to tasting room.*

EBERLE WINERY

Paso Robles

In Napa Valley, well-known names like Mondavi and Beringer are among those credited with helping to establish that region's wine industry. While the name Gary Eberle might not be as recognizable, the burgeoning Paso Robles wine industry was shaped in large part by the pioneering efforts of Gary and a handful of others during the early 1980s. It was this commitment and foresight that helped focus renewed attention on the region's winemaking potential and has resulted in a steady stream of new winery openings over the past decade or so.

Gary, a former defensive tackle under Joe Paterno at Penn State, came by his expertise as a longtime student of science, earning a

master's degree in zoology and completing course work for two doctorates. One was in cytogenetics at Louisiana State University and the other was in enology and viticulture at the University of California, Davis.

After leaving Davis in 1973, Gary was asked to help establish Estrella Winery in Paso Robles, effectively pioneering what was then a relatively untapped viticultural area. Later, armed with a breadth of experience in winery and vineyard operations, Gary set out on his own. In 1984 he and his wife,

Jeanie, opened Eberle Winery in a wood-sided facility perched on a hill a few miles east of town.

In his intensive studies of local weather and soils, Gary realized the Paso Robles area was extremely well suited to Cabernet Sauvignon, and he has spent years perfecting the varietal. The Eberle Cabernet Sauvignon has been a consistent medal winner at major wine contests throughout the state.

The Eberle tasting room is one of the region's best. In addition to boasting a grand vineyard view, the tasting room offers a convenient view of the winemaking operation. Through one window, visitors can see the fermentation tanks and rows of oak barrels stacked a half-dozen high. A window at the other end of the room looks out over the outdoor crushing pad.

In addition to what Gary calls a "short and serious" list of varietals, Eberle produces a fruity blush called Eye of the Swine, the most unusually named wine in Southern California.

THE WINE LIST
Chardonnay
Eye of the Swine blush wine
Muscat Canelli
Barbera
Cabernet Sauvignon
Syrah
Zinfandel

VINTNER'S CHOICES
WHITE: *Chardonnay*
RED: *Cabernet Sauvignon*

EBERLE WINERY
HIGHWAY 46 EAST
PASO ROBLES, CA 93447
(805) 238-9607

HOURS: *Winter hours, 10 a.m.-5 p.m. daily; summer hours, 10 a.m.-6 p.m. daily*
TASTINGS: *Yes*
CHARGE FOR TASTING: *No*
TOURS: *By appointment*
PICNIC AREA: *Yes*
RETAIL SALES: *Yes*

DIRECTIONS: *From Highway 101 in Paso Robles, drive east on Highway 46 for three-and-a-half miles to winery on left.*

ARCIERO WINERY

Paso Robles

*T*hose who still question the Paso Robles area's serious commitment to wine production need only visit Arciero Winery for proof. This expansive wine estate, producing more than sixty-five-thousand cases per year, is impressive by any standards.

Brothers Phil and Frank Arciero, partners in one of California's largest construction and development companies, are used to building major projects, and their winery is no exception. One of the largest in Southern California, Arciero Winery appears long and low from the highway. Upon closer inspection, however, visitors will dis-

cover a huge facility cut deep into a hillside. The production area is a cool fourteen feet underground, and aging areas can accommodate up to 1.2 million gallons.

We suggest visitors first get a feel for the winery by taking the self-guided tour that starts just inside the grand, double-door entry on the lower level. From here you'll ascend the stairs and walk along carpeted hallways for a bird's eye view of fermentation tanks, French oak barrels, and modern crushing equipment. The tour ends with a view of the Arciero bottling line.

After seeing the production part of the winery, it's time for a taste or two of some of Arciero's many estate wines. Samples are poured in a large visitors center reached by a walkway that cuts through an expanse of lawn. There's also a gift shop and delicatessen here.

It's in the visitors center that you'll glimpse another side to the Arciero family. In one corner is a display of sleek race cars sponsored over the years by winery founder Frank Arciero, Sr. The retired autos include one from the 1984 Indianapolis 500.

THE WINE LIST
Chardonnay
Chenin Blanc
La Venera White
Muscat Canelli
Sauvignon Blanc
White Zinfandel
Cabernet Sauvignon
La Venera Red
Nebbiolo
Petite Sirah
Zinfandel

VINTNER'S CHOICES
WHITE: *Chardonnay*
RED: *Nebbiolo*

ARCIERO WINERY
5625 EAST HIGHWAY 46
PASO ROBLES, CA 93447
(805) 239-2562

HOURS: *Winter hours, 10 a.m.-5 p.m. daily; summer hours, 10 a.m.-6 p.m. daily*
TASTINGS: *Yes*
CHARGE FOR TASTING: *No*
TOURS: *Self-guided*
PICNIC AREA: *Yes*
RETAIL SALES: *Yes*

DIRECTIONS: *From Highway 101 in Paso Robles, drive east on Highway 46 for five miles to winery on right.*

MERIDIAN VINEYARDS

Paso Robles

Commanding a beautiful vine- and oak-covered hill overlooking the valley, Meridian Vineyards is the first winery encountered by those approaching the Paso Robles region via Highway 46 from the Central Valley. Set among stately oaks and boasting an attractive façade made partially of stone, Meridian makes a favorable first impression.

There are no tours offered of the production areas of Meridian. The only behind-the-scenes glimpse visitors have is of the cavernous barrel storage area through cathedral windows behind the tasting room bar. While we found the tasting room at Meridian to be bright, immaculate, and inviting, we were just as impressed with the winery's outdoor spaces. A walkway winds through a lawn area dotted with oak trees, and strategically placed benches offer grand views of the vineyards and surrounding countryside.

THE WINE LIST
Cabernet Blanc
Chardonnay
Gewürztraminer
Sauvignon Blanc
Cabernet Sauvignon
Pinot Noir
Syrah
Zinfandel

VINTNER'S CHOICES
WHITE: *Chardonnay*
RED: *Syrah*

MERIDIAN VINEYARDS
7000 HIGHWAY 46 EAST
PASO ROBLES, CA 93447
(805) 237-6000

HOURS: *10 a.m.-5 p.m.*
Wednesday through Monday
TASTINGS: *Yes*
CHARGE FOR TASTING: *No*
TOURS: *No*
PICNIC AREA: *Yes*
RETAIL SALES: *Yes*

DIRECTIONS: *From Highway
101 in Paso Robles, exit east on
Highway 46 and drive seven
miles to winery on left.*

Although the winery doesn't divulge it's annual production, the
long driveway through hundreds of acres of vineyards and the
spacious facility offer a hint. This isn't among the area's smaller
operations. Not only does it utilize its own vast harvest, Meridian
purchases fruit from Santa Barbara County and from other area
vineyards to make some of its wines.

SAN LUIS OBISPO AREA

TO PASO ROBLES

SAN LUIS OBISPO

101

227

BIDDLE RANCH RD.

▼ EDNA VALLEY VINEYARD

101

PRICE CYN. RD.

CORBETT CYN. VINEYARDS
▼

HI MTN. RD.

TALLEY VINEYARDS
▼

PISMO BEACH ●

227

SAUCELITO CYN. VINEYARD
▼

ARROYO GRANDE

TO SANTA MARIA

EDNA VALLEY VINEYARD

San Luis Obispo

*D*on't come to Edna Valley Vineyard expecting a fancy tasting room or a well-stocked gift shop. While visitors are welcome on a daily basis, the folks here invest most of their energies in making great wine. Consequently, tastings tend to be informal, taking place at a bar set up in the bustling warehouse. The production areas are up close and personal.

One of the largest wineries in the south state, Edna Valley Vineyard produces some fifty-thousand cases each year. Edna Valley operates under a partnership with Paragon Vineyard, which supplies the grapes and owns the surrounding vineyard and half of the winery; Chalone Wine Group, which supplied all of the equipment for the winery, owns the other half. In fact, the Edna Valley facility, built in 1980, is a virtual duplicate of the Chalone Vineyard winery, only twice as large.

Edna Valley has provided grapes for Chalone wines since the mid-seventies, and also employs the same classical winemaking methods as Chalone, using barrels from the same cooper.

The Edna Valley is a designated Viticultural Area where consistently cool days allow thin-skinned grapes like Pinot Noir and Chardonnay to prosper. Even during the summer, when the mercury soars in the nearby Paso  Robles area, the Edna Valley boasts a cooling marine effect, encouraging the grapes to ripen slowly and consistently.

Paragon Vineyard owner Jack Niven, whose family had been major shareholders in the old Purity market chain in Northern California, started growing grapes in Edna Valley in 1973 after the supermarket outlets were sold.

While Chardonnay accounts for most of the winery's production, Edna Valley makes a critically acclaimed Pinot Noir. A Brut Sparkling Wine is sold only at the winery.

THE WINE LIST
Brut Sparkling Wine
Chardonnay
Vin Gris of Pinot Noir
Gamay
Pinot Noir

VINTNER'S CHOICES
WHITE: *Estate Chardonnay*
RED: *Reserve Pinot Noir*

EDNA VALLEY VINEYARD
2585 BIDDLE RANCH ROAD
SAN LUIS OBISPO, CA
93401
(805) 544-9594

HOURS: *10 a.m.-4 p.m. daily*
TASTINGS: *Yes*
CHARGE FOR TASTING: *No*
TOURS: *Yes*
PICNIC AREA: *Yes*
RETAIL SALES: *Yes*

DIRECTIONS: *From Highway 227 five miles southeast of San Luis Obispo, turn west on Biddle Ranch Road. Winery is on the right.*

EDNA VALLEY
VINEYARD
1991
Edna Valley
Pinot Noir
Vin Gris
Estate Bottled
Produced and bottled by
Edna Valley Vineyard
San Luis Obispo California USA
Alcohol 12.9% by volume

CORBETT CANYON VINEYARDS

San Luis Obispo

*A*s a rule of thumb, wineries tend to become smaller the farther one travels from California's main highways. In Edna Valley, however, we discovered the granddaddy of south coast wineries sitting far off the beaten track. So much for rules. At the time of our visit, Corbett Canyon Vineyards was producing some four-hundred-thousand cases per year. By comparison, neighboring Talley Vineyards makes less than five-thousand cases annually.

Corbett Canyon may be the largest winery in San Luis Obispo and Santa Barbara counties, but it's not without personality. The handsome plaster façade, arches, and tiled roof are reminiscent of the California mission

period. The spacious tasting room is well worth a visit, and tours of the hulking facility are offered. The giant-sized dejuicer, standing some three stories tall, is also an awesome sight.

Vineyards are conspicuously absent from Corbett Canyon's Edna Valley property. While the winery buys grapes from other growers in the San Luis Obispo area and nearby Santa Barbara region, the main grape source is its own six-hundred-acre vineyard near Santa Maria, just to the south. Corbett Canyon's Chardonnay and Pinot Noir fruit generally comes from the cool growing regions of Santa Barbara County and southern San Luis Obispo County, while the warmer Paso Robles area typically supplies Sauvignon Blanc, Zinfandel, and Cabernet Sauvignon grapes.

Owned by the Wine Group, which operates two other large winery properties, Corbett Canyon claims the largest number of awards of any winery in the south coast region.

THE WINE LIST
Chardonnay
Sauvignon Blanc
White Zinfandel
Cabernet Sauvignon
Merlot
Pinot Noir

VINTNER'S CHOICES
WHITE: *Reserve Chardonnay*
RED: *Coastal Classic Merlot*

CORBETT CANYON VINEYARDS
2195 CORBETT CANYON ROAD
SAN LUIS OBISPO, CA 93420
(805) 544-5800

HOURS: *10 a.m.-4:30 p.m. daily*
TASTINGS: *Yes*
CHARGE FOR TASTING: *No*
TOURS: *On weekends or weekdays by appointment*
PICNIC AREA: *Yes*
RETAIL SALES: *Yes*

DIRECTIONS: *From San Luis Obispo, drive south on Highway 227 for eight miles. Turn left on Corbett Canyon Road and drive one mile to winery on right.*

TALLEY VINEYARDS

Arroyo Grande

W̶ine buffs will enjoy a taste of history with a sample or two of Talley wines. The tasting room, which is depicted on the winery label, is the El Rincon Adobe, a regionally significant structure built in the early 1860s by one of the first settlers of the Arroyo Grande Valley. The charming cottage at the top of a small hill has been lovingly restored and now serves as the centerpiece of the property.

Picnic tables dot the lawn area around the adobe.

Although originally surrounded by fruit and olive trees, wheat, corn, and barley, the adobe now presides over more than seventy acres of vineyards. The Talley family, which operates the business, tends an approximate total of one-hundred acres on three sites.

The Talleys have been making wine only since 1986, but the family has deep roots in the local agricultural community. Oliver Talley started Talley Farms by growing specialty vegetables in the Arroyo Grande Valley in 1948. Oliver's son Don, convinced of the potential for growing wine grapes, planted a small test plot in 1982 on the steep hillsides above the vegetable fields. Experts from the University of California, Davis, were called in to help refine the varietal and clonal selections of Chardonnay and Pinot Noir, and planting began in earnest. In the meantime, Don's son Brian has become involved in the operation. Talley wines are made in an eighty-five-hundred-square-foot winery that sits behind the adobe at the foot of the Rincon Vineyard.

THE WINE LIST
Chardonnay
Sauvignon Blanc
White Riesling
Pinot Noir

VINTNER'S CHOICES
WHITE: *Chardonnay*
RED: *Pinot Noir*

TALLEY VINEYARDS
3031 LOPEZ DRIVE
ARROYO GRANDE, CA 93420
(805) 489-0446

HOURS: *Winter hours,*
11 a.m.-5 p.m. Thursday through
Sunday; summer hours,
11 a.m.-5 p.m. daily
TASTINGS: *Yes*
CHARGE FOR TASTING: *No*
TOURS: *No*
PICNIC AREA: *Yes*
RETAIL SALES: *Yes*

DIRECTIONS: *From Highway*
101 in Arroyo Grande, exit at
Lopez Drive and drive west
approximately five miles to winery
on left.

SAUCELITO CANYON VINEYARD

Arroyo Grande

In restoring a small, century-old Zinfandel vineyard in the upper Arroyo Grande Valley in 1974, Bill and Nancy Greenough also gave new life to an interesting family story as old as the vines.

The Greenoughs' Saucelito Canyon Vineyard was originally part of Rancho Saucelito, a sprawling ranch homesteaded in 1878 by Englishman Henry Ditmas and his wife, Rosa. It was Henry who cleared the property and planted grapevines—mostly Muscat and Zinfandel—imported from France and Spain.

After a divorce in 1886, Henry left the ranch and Rosa married the man next door, A. B. Hasbrouck, who also owned a vineyard and operated a winery. The couple continued to market wines for many years until tragedy struck with a double whammy in 1915. Phylloxera destroyed much of the Hasbrouck vineyard, and Rosa lost her husband. Rosa and her son Cecil kept the winery in operation with

grapes from Rancho Saucelito, but closed the business just before Prohibition. However, the remoteness of Rancho Saucelito attracted bootleggers who tended the vines and made illegal wine on site throughout the Prohibition years.

Not too long after Rosa's death in 1927, the winery and vineyard were finally abandoned. When Cecil died, Rancho Saucelito was passed to his daughters, who in turn sold the vineyard to the Greenoughs.

Bill toiled for months clearing the overgrown land, retraining each of the old head-pruned vines, and planting new vines. His vineyard now consists of the original three acres of Zinfandel, another few new acres of the varietal, a couple of acres of Cabernet Sauvignon, and a small plot of Sauvignon Blanc. All grow without irrigation.

The winery is a modest, wood-sided structure that still has no electricity. Inside are small barrels and fermentation tanks sufficient to produce about two-thousand cases per year. Although production is limited, Saucelito Canyon's wines have earned medals every year.

Wine enthusiasts who aren't up to the ride into Arroyo Grande Valley may taste Saucelito Canyon Vineyard's wares at Talley Vineyards ten miles away.

THE WINE LIST
Cabernet Sauvignon
Zinfandel

VINTNER'S CHOICE
RED: *Zinfandel*

SAUCELITO CANYON VINEYARD
1600 SAUCELITO CREEK ROAD
ARROYO GRANDE, CA 93420
(805) 489-8762

HOURS: *By appointment*
TASTINGS: *By appointment*
CHARGE FOR TASTING: *No*
TOURS: *By appointment*
PICNIC AREA: *By appointment*
RETAIL SALES: *By appointment*

DIRECTIONS: *The winery is located on a private locked road off Hi Mountain Road, just past Lopez Lake. Call winery for an appointment and specific directions.*

SANTA MARIA TO OAKVIEW

TO SANTA MARIA

BETTERAVIA ROAD

SANTA MARIA
MESA RD.

TEPUSQUET ROAD

▾ BYRON VINEYARD
AND WINERY

101

▾ RANCHO SISQUOC WINERY

▾ FOXEN VINEYARD

FOXEN CANYON ROAD

ALISOS
CYN. RD.

▾ ZACA MESA WINERY

FIRESTONE ▾ FESS PARKER WINERY
VINEYARD ▾

◀ ZACA STATION ROAD

FOXEN CANYON
ROAD

BABCOCK
VINEYARDS
▾

LOS OLIVOS

246 BUELLTON

CAREY ▾ THE BRANDER
▾ HOUTZ VINEYARD

SAN MARCOS
PASS

SANTA ROSA ROAD

GAINEY ▾
VINEYARD

101

101

154

▾
SANFORD
WINERY

SANTA BARBARA
TO VENTURA/OAKVIEW

BYRON VINEYARD AND WINERY

Santa Maria

*A*graduate degree in enology, a successful eight-year stint as winemaker at acclaimed Zaca Mesa, proprietor of his own award-winning winery... it's hard to believe that youthful-looking Byron "Ken" Brown hasn't always been a vintner. Truth is, he's been around the block a couple of times. A native of Sacramento, Ken served time in two earlier careers, first as an IBM salesman and then as a real estate developer. It wasn't until he planted a small personal vineyard at his home in the foothills above Sacramento that Ken discovered his true calling. In this case, the third time was indeed the charm.

In 1974, nearly a decade after earning a degree in business administration from Linfield College, Ken shuttered his real estate enterprise and enrolled in the graduate enology program at California State University, Fresno. A college research project took him to Santa Barbara County just as the local wine industry was beginning to blossom. It was here that he met Marshall Ream, who built Zaca Mesa Winery and hired Ken as his winemaker.

After eight years with Zaca Mesa, Ken struck out on his own and with his wife, Deborah, created his namesake winery in the Tepusquet Canyon area of Santa Maria.

The winery occupies a small oasis at the edge of wild canyonland.

After a sample or two in the tasting room, visitors may linger at a shaded outdoor table and savor the rugged beauty of the valley with a glass of Byron wine.

Byron's six-hundred-forty-one-acre property includes the respected Nielson Vineyard, the county's oldest commercial grape plot, planted over three decades ago. Just over half of the winery's annual production is Chardonnay. Pinot Noir represents about thirty percent. A self-described "Pinot Noir fanatic," Ken produces this wine according to the traditional Burgundian technique. He uses small open-top fermenters to ensure maximum color and flavor. He bottles the best vineyard lots as Pinot Noir Reserve.

Producing about twenty-five-thousand cases per year at the time of our visit, the winery is expected to double in output by the year 2000. In 1990, Byron Vineyard and Winery was acquired by the Robert Mondavi Winery, but Ken continues to run the business independently.

THE WINE LIST
Chardonnay
Pinot Blanc
Sauvignon Blanc
Cabernet Sauvignon
Pinot Noir

VINTNER'S CHOICES
WHITE: *Chardonnay*
RED: *Pinot Noir*

BYRON VINEYARD AND WINERY
5230 TEPUSQUET ROAD
SANTA MARIA, CA 93454
(805) 937-7288

HOURS: *10 a.m.-4 p.m. daily*
TASTINGS: *Yes*
CHARGE FOR TASTING: *No*
TOURS: *Yes*
PICNIC AREA: *Yes*
RETAIL SALES: *Yes*

DIRECTIONS: *From Highway 101, exit at Betteravia Road and drive east for six miles. Take the left fork and follow Santa Maria Mesa Road for five miles. At the end of the road and stop sign, bear left onto Tepusquet Road, and follow to winery on the right.*

RANCHO SISQUOC WINERY

Santa Maria

*H*aving *already discovered a local winery owned by actor Fess Parker, and one operated by a member of the Firestone Tire and Rubber clan, we weren't particularly surprised to learn that Rancho Sisquoc Winery is the property of another famous family: the James Floods of San Francisco, descendants of the founder of Wells Fargo Bank.*

Part of a thirty-seven-thousand-acre land grant that's still intact, Rancho Sisquoc is primarily a cattle ranch. And even though wine-making is secondary (only about six-thousand cases are produced

annually), the ranch has some four-hundred acres of vineyards, making it one of the region's largest grape growers.

The winery's label depicts the little San Ramon chapel, a century-old church that sits along Foxen Canyon Road near the entrance to Rancho Sisquoc. A two-mile-long drive skirts the vineyards and crosses cattle guards, dead-ending at the ranch compound, a collection of tidy barns and houses nestled under ancient oaks. Among these is the winery tasting room, a small, rustic, barn like building. Inside, visitors cozy up to an antique bar with a brass rail.

Among Rancho Sisquoc's products is Franken Riesling, also known as Sylvaner, a white wine of German origin. Often used in blending, Franken Riesling isn't widely made in California.

THE WINE LIST
Chardonnay
Franken Riesling
Johannisberg Riesling
Sauvignon Blanc
Cabernet Sauvignon
Merlot

VINTNER'S CHOICES
WHITE: *Chardonnay*
RED: *Merlot*

RANCHO SISQUOC WINERY
6600 FOXEN CANYON ROAD
SANTA MARIA, CA 93454
(805) 934-4332

HOURS: *10 a.m.-4 p.m. daily*
TASTINGS: *Yes*
CHARGE FOR TASTING: *No*
TOURS: *On request*
PICNIC AREA: *Yes*
RETAIL SALES: *Yes*

DIRECTIONS: *From Highway 101, exit at Betteravia Road in Santa Maria. Betteravia Road becomes Foxen Canyon Road. Drive eighteen miles to winery drive on left. From Highway 154 just west of Los Olivos, drive north on Foxen Canyon Road for eighteen miles to winery drive on right.*

FOXEN VINEYARD

Santa Maria

The roots of the Foxen grapevines themselves don't run as deep as those of proprietor Dick Dore, whose great, great grandfather, Benjamin Foxen, was deeded this property in 1837 as part of a Spanish land grant. In fact, it was Dick's great grandmother who over a century ago built the old wood-sided and tin-roofed blacksmith shop and barn that today serves as the barrel and tasting room. The old storage barn was also constructed by Dick's ancestors.

While the property has been in the family for ages, Dick hasn't always called the ranch home. He gave up a promising Los Angeles banking career after feeling the urge to create a winery on the old homestead. In 1987, Dick teamed with Bill Wathen, a local vineyard manager, and together they bottled five-hundred cases, about one-tenth of their current production.

An estate vineyard of about eleven acres provides grapes for Chardonnay, Cabernet Sauvignon, Cabernet Franc, and Merlot. Fruit for Foxen's Pinot Noir and Chenin Blanc comes from vines in the Santa Maria Valley. Through what they describe as proper farming techniques, Bill and Dick were among the first Santa Barbara County winemakers to overcome the herbaceous and vegetal taste that for years plagued the region's Cabernet Sauvignon.

THE WINE LIST
Chardonnay
Chenin Blanc
Bordeaux blend
Cabernet Franc
Cabernet Sauvignon
Merlot
Pinot Noir

VINTNER'S CHOICES
WHITE: *Chardonnay*
RED: *Cabernet Sauvignon*

FOXEN VINEYARD
ROUTE 1, BOX 144A
FOXEN CANYON ROAD
SANTA MARIA, CA 93454
(805) 937-4251

HOURS: *12 Noon-4 p.m.*
Saturday and Sunday
TASTINGS: *Yes*
CHARGE FOR TASTING: *No*
TOURS: *By appointment*
PICNIC AREA: *Yes*
RETAIL SALES: *Yes*

DIRECTIONS: *From Highway
101, exit at Betteravia Road in
Santa Maria. Betteravia Road
becomes Foxen Canyon Road.
Drive past Rancho Sisquoc
entrance; Foxen's small winery
barn is just off the left side of
road. There is no prominent sign
or address. From Highway 154
just west of Los Olivos, drive
north on Foxen Canyon Road for
fifteen miles to winery on right.*

Since Dick and Bill are responsible for the entire operation, there's not a lot of time for entertaining visitors. Consequently, the winery is open only eight hours a week, from noon until four, Saturdays and Sundays. Make sure you plan your weekend travels accordingly. This is not one to be missed.

ZACA MESA WINERY

Los Olivos

The Santa Ynez Valley's northernmost winery, Zaca Mesa, has been turning out wines for more than two decades. Since the region's premium wine industry didn't gather steam until the mid-to-late seventies, Zaca Mesa is among the patriarchs.

The winery was founded in 1972 by a number of farsighted business associates, among them John C. Cushman, III, a high-rise office building developer. John later bought out his colleagues and is now Zaca Mesa's sole proprietor.

At the time of our visit, Zaca Mesa's Reserve Chardonnay, Reserve Pinot Noir, and Syrah had all recently earned gold medals at the

prestigious Orange County Fair wine judging, as well as numerous other awards. The winery's Reserve Chardonnay and Reserve Pinot Noir are released in late spring; Syrah is released in mid-spring. Premium Chardonnay is available year-round.

The spacious tasting room at Zaca Mesa, with its bucolic views, is among the most inviting in the region. The winery forms a horseshoe around an oak-shaded lawn and a covered picnic area. Chilled wines and cheese and crackers are sold at the tasting room. Tours leave every half-hour and include a walk through the winery's production facility, which bulges with hundreds and hundreds of oak barrels, rows of open-topped fermenters, and overhead dejuicing tanks.

THE WINE LIST
Chardonnay
Johannisberg Riesling
Late Harvest Riesling
Pinot Noir
Syrah

VINTNER'S CHOICES
WHITE: *Chardonnay*
RED: *Pinot Noir*

ZACA MESA WINERY
6905 FOXEN CANYON
ROAD
LOS OLIVOS, CA 93441
(805) 688-9339

HOURS: *10 a.m.-4 p.m. daily*
TASTINGS: *Yes*
CHARGE FOR TASTING: *No*
TOURS: *Yes*
PICNIC AREA: *Yes*
RETAIL SALES: *Yes*

DIRECTIONS: *The winery is located approximately eight miles from Highway 101. From the south, exit at Zaca Station Road near Los Olivos and follow to winery on left. From the north, exit at Alisos Canyon Road in Los Alamos. At Foxen Canyon Road turn right and drive to winery on right.*

FESS PARKER WINERY

Los Olivos

*I*n the movie Davy Crockett, *Fess Parker's last stand was the Alamo. In real life it's a winery in Los Olivos.*

After successful careers in motion pictures and real estate development, at an age when most of us might be more content to pull up an easy chair, Fess established Fess Parker Winery along with his wife, Marcy, son, Eli (Fess Parker III), and daughter, Ashley. Residents of Santa Barbara since the 1960s, the Parkers watched as the region's premium wine industry burgeoned. Fess's family has roots in farming, and he decided to take the plunge himself. In 1987 he bought some land in the upper valley and began planting grapevines.

The winery, which opened in 1992, reflects colonial English architecture and is dominated by a metal roof that forms a wide veranda around the entire building.

At the time of our visit, about sixty acres of grapes were under cultivation on the seven-hundred-acre ranch, and plans were on the table to more than double the size of those vineyards. The Parkers hope ultimately to increase their operation to about forty-thousand cases per year, supplementing a traditional roster with Rhône varietals like Viognier and Marsanne, two white wines not usually associated with this region.

Despite the winery's tender age, the label with the coonskin cap has already appeared in some lofty circles. Former President Bush toasted former President Reagan with a Fess Parker Chardonnay at the opening of the Reagan library, and the same wine was poured at the 1991 wedding of Elizabeth Taylor and Larry Fortensky. For the latter event, the wine didn't have far to travel. The Taylor wedding was held at pop star Michael Jackson's Neverland estate, which is just over the hill from the winery.

THE WINE LIST
Chardonnay
Johannisberg Riesling
Muscat Canelli
Merlot
Pinot Noir
Syrah

VINTNER'S CHOICES
WHITE: *Johannisberg Riesling*
RED: *Pinot Noir*

FESS PARKER WINERY
6200 FOXEN CANYON ROAD
LOS OLIVOS, CA 93441
(805) 688-1545 OR TOLL-FREE
(800) 841-1104

HOURS: *10 a.m.-4 p.m. daily*
TASTINGS: *Yes*
CHARGE FOR TASTING: *Yes*
TOURS: *No*
PICNIC AREA: *Yes*
RETAIL SALES: *Yes*

DIRECTIONS: *From Highway 101 between Los Alamos and Buellton, exit north on Zaca Station Road and drive five miles to winery on right.*

FIRESTONE VINEYARD

Los Olivos

*A*t age thirty-five, he was high on the corporate career ladder, ensconced in a plush London office as head of British operations for his family's Firestone Tire and Rubber Company. There was just one problem. Brooks Firestone wanted out.

Although both his father and grandfather had been company men, the rubber business wasn't Brooks' calling. So in 1971 he resigned from the company and made a serendipitous decision to leave

London, moving his growing family to California, where he had spent his childhood. Around that time, Brooks was dispatched to the Santa Ynez Valley to take a look at four-hundred acres of land, including over one-hundred acres of vineyards, that had recently been purchased by his father. Both Brooks and his wife, Kate, fell in love with the valley.

After a review of soil and climate research that confirmed the region's potential for growing premium wine grapes, Brooks knew he had found his niche. In 1973 he began growing additional vines and two years later work started on the winery. Despite the fact that a couple of other commercial vintners were already in operation in 1975, Brooks is generally credited with bringing premium winemaking to the Santa Ynez Valley. Today, Firestone Vineyard is the area's largest winery, producing over seventy-five-thousand cases per year.

Noted winery architect Richard Keith, who created Napa Valley's striking Sterling winery, designed the equally impressive Firestone facility. The winery's angular roofline caught our eye from miles away as we made our way above the valley along Foxen Canyon Road from Los Olivos. Resembling what might best be described as folded wings, the building stands on a knoll against a backdrop of oak-studded hills surrounded by some two-hundred-sixty acres of vines.

Guests enter through heavy wooden doors that open onto a lush courtyard with gravel walkways, picnic tables, and a tiled fountain. The hacienda theme is carried into the tasting room, which is decorated with Latin American art.

THE WINE LIST
Chardonnay
Gewürztraminer
Johannisberg Riesling
Sauvignon Blanc
Cabernet Sauvignon
Merlot
Red table wine

VINTNER'S CHOICES
WHITE: *Johannisberg Riesling*
RED: *Merlot*

FIRESTONE VINEYARD
5017 ZACA STATION ROAD
LOS OLIVOS, CA 93441
(805) 688-3940

HOURS: *10 a.m.-4 p.m. daily*
TASTINGS: *Yes*
CHARGE FOR TASTING:
*No; charge for groups of
15 or more*
TOURS: *Yes*
PICNIC AREA: *Yes*
RETAIL SALES: *Yes*

DIRECTIONS: *From Highway
101 between Los Alamos and
Buellton, exit north on Zaca
Station Road and drive two-and-
a-half miles to winery on left.*

THE BRANDER VINEYARD

Los Olivos

*H*aving *planted a vineyard of Bordeaux varietals, Fred Brander took the next authentic step in establishing his namesake winery. He built a château-style winery flanked by twin towers, creating a little bit of France in the middle of Santa Ynez Valley.*

From the outside, the château strikes a formal French pose. However, tastings are very informal. Samples are poured at a simple table by friendly staffers while breezes flow through open French doors. A sunny patio affords a view of the surrounding vines.

To the left of the tasting room is a long dark room where Brander vintages age in new French oak barrels. About seven-thousand cases are made each year.

Fred's vineyard, planted in 1975, includes about eight acres of Cabernet Sauvignon, six acres of Merlot, and three acres of Cabernet

Franc. Brander's Bouchet Meritage is a blend of these grapes, with Cabernet playing the dominant role. In the spring, the winery offers a "futures" program through which customers may purchase yet-to-be-bottled Bouchet at considerable savings a few months prior to the actual release date.

THE WINE LIST
Chardonnay
Sauvignon Blanc
Bouchet
Merlot
Pinot Noir

VINTNER'S CHOICES
WHITE: *Sauvignon Blanc*
RED: *Bouchet*

THE BRANDER VINEYARD
2401 REFUGIO ROAD
LOS OLIVOS, CA 93441
(805) 688-2455

HOURS: *10 a.m.-5 p.m. daily*
TASTINGS: *Yes*
CHARGE FOR TASTING: *No*
TOURS: *No*
PICNIC AREA: *Yes*
RETAIL SALES: *Yes*

DIRECTIONS: *From Highway 154 just south of Los Olivos, turn east on Roblar Avenue to winery drive on left.*

Although Brander makes Bouchet (also known as Cabernet Franc), Chardonnay, Merlot, and Pinot Noir, Fred's primary wine is Sauvignon Blanc. So proud of this wine is Fred that he once delivered a case to the nearby ranch of former president Ronald Reagan. In a thank-you phone call from the president, Fred learned that an earlier Brander Sauvignon Blanc vintage had been shared with another head of state who likely knew a thing or two about quality wines: French President François Mitterrand. Mr. Reagan reported that the wine was a hit.

THE GAINEY VINEYARD

Santa Ynez

*A*lthough he achieved professional success as president of the Jostens corporation and as the head of one of the nation's top Arabian horse breeding farms, Daniel Gainey isn't one to rest on his laurels. He and his wife, Robin, are already well on their way to yet another professional success in winemaking with The Gainey Vineyard.

In operation for little more than a decade, The Gainey Vineyard has become a must-stop on any Santa Ynez winery tour. Nestled at the center of a well-kept vineyard, the winery has the appearance of a Spanish-style estate, with bright white plaster walls and red tile roof. Inside are weathered Mexican tiles as well as antique treasures from

throughout Europe. In our opinion it's the most handsome winery in the entire region.

The Gainey Vineyard represents but a piece of the vast eighteen-hundred-acre Gainey Ranch that the family founded in 1962. The Santa Ynez Valley's largest diversified farming operation, Gainey Ranch includes one of the oldest Arabian horse breeding farms in the United States, Gainey Fountainhead Arabians. In 1982, Daniel began translating to blueprints his longtime dream of creating a premium winery. The opening of The Gainey Vineyard two years later coincided with Daniel's retirement from Jostens.

In addition to creating thirteen-thousand cases of award-winning varietals each year, the Gaineys have created a cultural magnet with their attractive winery. The vineyard is the site of a year-round program of wine and food appreciation classes, a summer concert series, and changing art exhibits.

THE WINE LIST
Chardonnay
Johannisberg Riesling
Late Harvest Johannisberg Riesling
Sauvignon Blanc
Cabernet Sauvignon
Merlot
Pinot Noir

VINTNER'S CHOICES
WHITE: *Sauvignon Blanc*
RED: *Pinot Noir*

THE GAINEY VINEYARD
3950 EAST HIGHWAY 246
SANTA YNEZ, CA 93460
(805) 688-0558

HOURS: *10 a.m.-5 p.m. daily*
TASTINGS: *Yes*
CHARGE FOR TASTING: *Yes*
TOURS: *Yes*
PICNIC AREA: *Yes*
RETAIL SALES: *Yes*

DIRECTIONS: *From north-bound Highway 101, exit at Highway 154 in Santa Barbara and follow over the San Marcos Pass to Highway 246 near Santa Ynez. Turn left on Highway 246 and drive a half-mile to winery on left. From southbound Highway 101, exit at Highway 246 near Buellton and drive east. Winery is three miles past Solvang on the right.*

CAREY CELLARS

Solvang

$\mathscr{B}$*rooks and Kate Firestone are a dual winery couple. Firestone Vineyard is his; Carey Cellars is hers.*

An accomplished soloist with Britain's Sadler's Wells Ballet in her younger years, Kate moved with her family to the United States in the early 1970s after London-based Brooks had a peek at some property purchased by his father in the Santa Ynez Valley. Convinced the land was perfect for growing grapes, Brooks said goodbye to a senior executive career with his family's Firestone Tire and Rubber company

to found Firestone Vineyard. In 1988, after getting Firestone Vineyard up and running, the family bought nearby Carey Cellars. Brooks suggested that Kate run it, and she accepted the challenge.

Carey Cellars is an attractive property whose centerpiece is a weathered red barn. Transformed from a dairy to a winery

in 1978 by original owner Dr. J. Campbell Carey, the winery turns out only about ten-thousand cases per year.

Next to the barn, a tidy bungalow-style home now functions as the tasting room and gift shop. At the time of our visit, another Kate—the proprietor's daughter-in-law—was hosting visitors.

Among Carey's more noteworthy wines is Arabesque, a blend of forty-percent Cabernet Sauvignon, forty-percent Merlot, and twenty-percent Cabernet Franc. According to Kate the wine is "blended to be approachable within a few years of release, but to gain in complexity for many years." The Cabernet and Merlot grapes that compose Arabesque are taken from nearby La Cuesta Vineyard, regarded by locals as one of the finest vineyards in the region.

THE WINE LIST
Chardonnay
Muscat
Pinot Noir Blanc
Sauvignon Blanc
Arabesque
Cabernet Sauvignon
Merlot

VINTNER'S CHOICES
WHITE: *Chardonnay*
RED: *La Cuesta Cabernet Reserve*

CAREY CELLARS
1711 ALAMO PINTADO ROAD
SOLVANG, CA 93463
(805) 688-8554

HOURS: *10 a.m.-4 p.m. daily*
TASTINGS: *Yes*
CHARGE FOR TASTING: *No*
TOURS: *Yes*
PICNIC AREA: *Yes*
RETAIL SALES: *Yes*

DIRECTIONS: *From Highway 101, exit at Highway 154 and drive to Los Olivos. Turn south on Grand Avenue and proceed through town. Turn south onto Alamo Pintado Road to winery on right.*

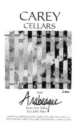

HOUTZ VINEYARDS

Los Olivos

After years in busy careers in the Los Angeles area, she as a systems analyst and he in real estate, Margy and Dave Houtz went searching for a little peace and comfort. They found and nurtured it in the Santa Ynez Valley, at a place they call Peace and Comfort Farm. The two lambs featured on the winery's label are intended to symbolize the Bach cantata "Sheep May Safely Graze," which inspired the farm's name.

Now the home of Houtz Vineyards, the former cattle ranch is about as peaceful and comfortable as they get. Along one side of the winery drive, vineyards sweep into the distance. On the other side, families of ducks and geese share a pond while a couple of wine tasters watch from a cozy gazebo. And all around are roses—some two-hundred varieties.

Dave and Margy, who in addition to making wine also find time to grow apples commercially, started Houtz Vineyards in 1984. Production hasn't skyrocketed over the years. Rather, the couple prefers to keep it small. Only about three-thousand cases are produced each year, making Houtz one of the region's smaller wineries.

Less than half of the farm's forty acres are given to vineyards. We have a personal favorite among the Houtz line in the popular Sauvignon Blanc, a smoky-tasting wine that spends its aging time in small French oak barrels. This is the perfect wine to enjoy with your picnic lunch near the Houtz pond. Chilled bottles are available at the tasting room inside the little red winery.

THE WINE LIST
Chardonnay
Sauvignon Blanc
Cabernet Sauvignon

VINTNER'S CHOICES
WHITE: *Sauvignon Blanc*
RED: *Cabernet Sauvignon*

HOUTZ VINEYARDS
2670 ONTIVEROS ROAD
LOS OLIVOS, CA 93441
(805) 688-8664

HOURS: *12 Noon-4 p.m.*
Friday through Sunday
TASTINGS: *Yes*
CHARGE FOR TASTING: *No*
TOURS: *No*
PICNIC AREA: *Yes*
RETAIL SALES: *Yes*

DIRECTIONS: *From Highway 101, exit at Highway 154 and drive to Los Olivos. Turn south on Grand Avenue and proceed through town. Bear left up the hill and continue on Roblar Avenue. Turn right on Exterior Road and follow signs to winery.*

SANFORD WINERY

Buellton

Maybe it was the vivid mustard-colored walls against an indigo summer sky. Perhaps it was the sultry breeze that swirled about the tasting room from windows without glass. Whatever it was cast a mystical spell on us that lingered for months. We can't explain exactly why, but Sanford was our favorite Southern California tasting room.

The adobe-walled production facility had yet to be completed at the time of our visit, and wines were still being made at an industrial complex in nearby Buellton. Visitors are welcomed at the rustic tasting room at the end of a dusty road five miles west of Highway 101.

Proprietors Richard and Thekla Sanford fashioned this unusual facility from an old dairy farm. Weatherbeaten material from the old ranch buildings were used to create the tasting room and office. A waist-high foundation of mustard-colored concrete is topped with old

barn wood. A simple tin roof covers the structure.

Inside the tasting room is a half-circle-shaped pine bar on a tiled floor. Bookshelves line one wall, and a plain wooden table with four chairs sits at the room's center. Because the large windows have no glass and doors are open, the room

exudes a friendly, open, and airy feel. During the cooler months a woodburning stove provides heat.

A former yachtsman and naval navigator, Richard opened Sanford Winery in 1981. Although the Sanford holdings total over seven-hundred acres, only about twenty-five were planted to vines at the time of our visit. Richard relies on purchases from other vineyards in the region to produce about thirty-thousand cases per year.

In addition to award-winning Pinot Noir, Chardonnay, and Sauvignon Blanc, Sanford makes a reasonably priced blush Pinot Vin Gris from Pinot Noir grapes.

By the way, Sanford's labels are among the southland's most beautiful. Each year they feature a different series of wildflowers, created by famed wine label artist Sebastian Titus.

THE WINE LIST
Chardonnay
Pinot Noir Vin Gris
Sauvignon Blanc
Pinot Noir

VINTNER'S CHOICES
WHITE: *Chardonnay*
RED: *Pinot Noir*

SANFORD WINERY
7250 SANTA ROSA ROAD
BUELLTON, CA 93427
(805) 688-3300

HOURS: *11 a.m.-4 p.m. daily*
TASTINGS: *Yes*
CHARGE FOR TASTING: *No*
TOURS: *No*
PICNIC AREA: *Yes*
RETAIL SALES: *Yes*

DIRECTIONS: *From Highway 101, exit at Santa Rosa Road at Buellton and drive west for five miles to winery drive on left.*

BABCOCK VINEYARDS

Lompoc

*T*he westernmost winery in the Santa Ynez Valley Appellation District, Babcock Vineyards is our award-winner for the region's most remote destination. Consequently, it's a great discovery, especially for those who don't enjoy weekend wine-tasting crowds at the wineries nearer to the valley's heart.

The roots of this family winery, which opened in 1984, can be traced to Walt and Mona Babcock's longtime involvement in the restaurant business. Owners of Walt's Wharf in Seal Beach and Oysters in Corona del Mar, the couple learned so much about wine over the

years that they bought some land and planted a vineyard. The resulting grapes were of such good quality that the family took the next step of building a winery. Their son, Bryan, became the winemaker.

The small, barn-style building, which contains both the aging facilities and tasting room, is situated near brilliant flower fields, providing visitors with a colorful bonus. The winery is located about midway between Highways One and 101. It's about a twenty-minute drive from Solvang.

At the time of our visit, the Babcock family was making preparations to grow what Bryan calls "fringe varietals," like Vernaccia, a Tuscan grape that makes a dry white wine. Experimenting with new wines is part of the Babcock philosophy of "having as much fun as possible, which is important because the wine business is very demanding and competitive."

THE WINE LIST
Chardonnay
Gewürztraminer
Riesling
Sauvignon Blanc
Pinot Noir

VINTNER'S CHOICES
WHITE: *Sauvignon Blanc*
RED: *Pinot Noir*

BABCOCK VINEYARDS
5175 HIGHWAY 246
LOMPOC, CA 93436
(805) 736-1455

HOURS: *10:30 a.m.-4 p.m. weekends, and by appointment weekdays*
TASTINGS: *Yes*
CHARGE FOR TASTING: *Yes*
TOURS: *By appointment*
PICNIC AREA: *Yes*
RETAIL SALES: *Yes*

DIRECTIONS: *From Highway 101 at Buellton, drive northwest on Highway 246 for nine-and-a-half miles to winery on right.*

OLD CREEK RANCH WINERY

Oakview

*A*lthough the century-old winery, the oldest in Ventura County, had fallen into disrepair, and there were no grapes growing on the property, Carmel Maitland wasn't dissuaded from reviving the winemaking tradition of Old Creek Ranch. Carmel and her husband, John (Mike) Maitland, an executive with MCA, bought the ranch in the wooded foothills above Ventura in 1976, ostensibly as an early retirement project. Unfortunately, Mike died not long after the purchase, and Carmel found herself sole owner of an eight-

hundred-fifty-acre cattle ranch and a decrepit, turn-of-the-century winery that hadn't been used since the 1940s.

In 1980, a home-winemaking friend suggested that Carmel give some thought to reestablishing a winery on the ranch. As a lark, she bought some grapes from area vineyards, invited a couple of winemaking hobbyists to the property, and crushed the fruit in some small tubs. Recycled bottles were filled with what was the label's first vintage of less than five-hundred cases. The following year, a three-family partnership was formed and winemaking officially returned to Old Creek Ranch.

It wasn't long before new vineyards began growing, and a modern production facility was constructed near the original wood and stone winery, whose picture is on the label. Visitors are received in a cozy tasting room with a fireplace. The winery takes its grapes from about twelve acres of estate Sauvignon Blanc, Chenin Blanc, Cabernet Sauvignon, Merlot, and Chardonnay. Johannisberg Riesling grapes are purchased from Rancho Sisquoc in the Santa Ynez Valley. Between eighteen-hundred and two-thousand cases are made each year, and most is sold out of the tasting room.

Because of her responsibilities elsewhere on the sprawling cattle and horse ranch, Carmel is usually at the winery only during what she calls "long weekends," an arrangement that makes for some fairly inconsistent hours of operation. Other staff tend the operation during weekdays. You might want to call ahead, just to make sure the winery is open.

THE WINE LIST
Chardonnay
Chenin Blanc
Johannisberg Riesling
Sauvignon Blanc
Cabernet Sauvignon
   Merlot

VINTNER'S CHOICES
WHITE: *Johannisberg*
   Riesling
RED: *Merlot*

OLD CREEK RANCH WINERY
10024 OLD CREEK ROAD
OAKVIEW, CA 93022
(805) 649-4132

HOURS: *10 a.m.-5 p.m. Friday through Sunday*
TASTINGS: *Yes*
CHARGE FOR TASTING: *No*
TOURS: *Self-guided*
PICNIC AREA: *Yes*
RETAIL SALES: *Yes*

DIRECTIONS: *From Highway 101 in Ventura, drive east on Highway 33 through Casitas Springs toward Ojai. Turn right on Old Creek Road (at cider barn) and follow to winery at end of road.*

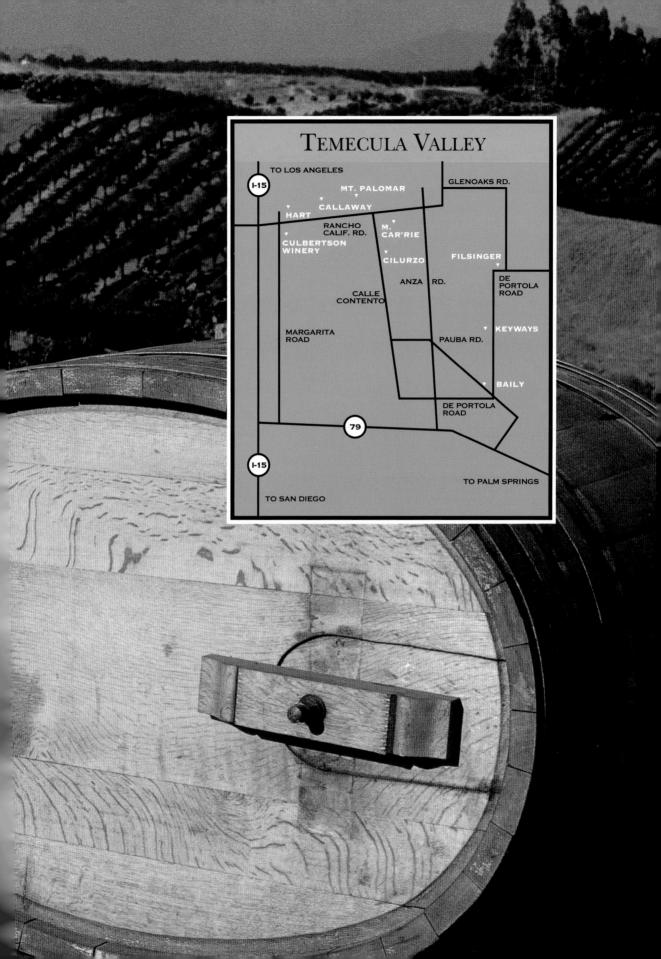

TEMECULA VALLEY

TO LOS ANGELES

I-15

GLENOAKS RD.

MT. PALOMAR

CALLAWAY

HART

RANCHO
CALIF. RD.

M.
CAR'RIE

CULBERTSON
WINERY

CILURZO

FILSINGER

ANZA RD.

DE
PORTOLA
ROAD

CALLE
CONTENTO

MARGARITA
ROAD

KEYWAYS

PAUBA RD.

BAILY

DE PORTOLA
ROAD

79

I-15

TO PALM SPRINGS

TO SAN DIEGO

HART WINERY

Temecula

In contrast to the formal elegance of Culbertson Winery, which unfolds on the other side of the valley, Hart Winery is a small, informal operation run by the husband-and-wife team of Travis and Nancy Hart. Travis, who combines his job of winemaker with a career as a local junior high school teacher, is one of the Temecula Valley's veteran vintners. The winery, which opened in 1980, is among the area's oldest. It's also one of the smallest, producing only about five-thousand cases per year. Much of it is sold to visitors who make the short trek up the dirt drive from Rancho California Road.

Situated on a hillside overlooking the valley, the winery is a simple, board-and-batten, barnlike building that houses both production equipment and tasting room. A couple of tree-shaded picnic tables out front offer sweeping views of the vineyards and valley.

Although it's a small operation, the Harts, with assistance from their son, Bill, produce an impressive array of wines. In addition to the standards, their roster includes Mourvèdre and Grenache, two varietals that thrive not only in the intense heat of France's Rhône Valley but in the warm Temecula Valley. The family also bottles Zinfandel, Zinfandel Blanc, and Chardonnay under the Dos Sabas label. These wines are created from an adjacent eight-acre vineyard owned by the Saba family.

THE WINE LIST
Chardonnay
Sauvignon Blanc
White Riesling
Zinfandel Blanc
Cabernet Sauvignon
Grenache
Merlot
Mourvèdre
Zinfandel

VINTNER'S CHOICES
WHITE: *Sauvignon Blanc*
RED: *Merlot*

HART WINERY
41300 AVENIDA BIONA
TEMECULA, CA 92589
(909) 676-6300

HOURS: *9 a.m.-4:30 p.m. daily*
TASTINGS: *Yes*
CHARGE FOR TASTING: *Yes*
TOURS: *By appointment*
PICNIC AREA: *Yes; small*
RETAIL SALES: *Yes*

DIRECTIONS: *From Interstate 15, exit east on Rancho California Road and drive four miles to winery on left. Temecula is ninety miles southeast of Los Angeles and sixty miles north of San Diego.*

CALLAWAY VINEYARD AND WINERY

Temecula

For south state residents interested in getting an orientation to winemaking and wine appreciation, this large-scale facility is a fine place to learn the ABCs of production and tasting. You'll also find Callaway situated conveniently near the traditional starting point for a Temecula Valley wine tour.

The winery takes its name from founder Ely Callaway, former president of Burlington Industries, who planted about 150 acres of vineyards here in 1969. In 1974, after leaving his corporate post to pursue the vintner's art, Callaway opened a winery on the site. Hiram Walker of Ontario, Canada, bought the winery in 1981. Allied Lyons, a London-based international food and beverage company, is the current owner.

One of the largest of our Southern California backroad wineries, Callaway produces about two-hundred-twenty-five-thousand cases per

year. For more than ten years the winery has concentrated on white wines. At the time of our visit, only one red, Cabernet Sauvignon, was being produced by Callaway.

Instead of turning visitors loose in the tasting room, the

THE WINE LIST
Blanc de Blanc sparkling wine
Chardonnay
Chenin Blanc
Fumé Blanc
Muscat Canelli
Pinot Gris
Sauvignon Blanc
White Riesling
Cabernet Sauvignon

VINTNER'S CHOICES
WHITE: *Calla-Lees*
    Chardonnay
RED: *Cabernet Sauvignon*

**CALLAWAY VINEYARD AND
WINERY
32720 RANCHO
CALIFORNIA ROAD
TEMECULA, CA 92589
(909) 676-4001**

HOURS: *10:30 a.m.-5 p.m. daily*
TASTINGS: *Yes*
CHARGE FOR TASTING: *Yes*
TOURS: *Yes*
PICNIC AREA: *Yes*
RETAIL SALES: *Yes*

DIRECTIONS: *From Interstate
15, exit east on Rancho
California Road and drive four
miles to winery on left. Temecula
is ninety miles southeast of Los
Angeles and sixty miles north of
San Diego.*

folks at Callaway do some hand-holding. Seated at tables, visitors are guided, lecture-style, through the tasting process by well-informed staff who discuss the relationship between certain wines and food. Samples of several wines are offered for a small fee.

One of the state's more environmentally sensitive winemaking enterprises, Callaway minimizes its use of insecticides by letting grasses grow between the vines. The grasses are home to helpful bugs that feed on leaf-damaging insects; plum trees sustain the beneficial insects during the winter. Herbicides aren't used because weeds are controlled mechanically, and the winery maintains vineyard perches for wild birds that prey upon grape- and vine-eating rodents. The winery conserves water by using drip irrigation, and even traded its freon-based refrigeration units for an ozone-layer-saving ammonia-based system.

CULBERTSON WINERY

Temecula

The Culbertsons' imposing winery and restaurant complex is probably the largest expression to date of optimism about the future of the burgeoning wine industry of Temecula. It's obvious the operators of this sprawling facility believe folks will be coming out here for some time.

The only south state wine producer specializing in méthode champenoise, Culbertson is also the region's most elegant winery. No motorist will be able to ignore the striking two-story French Mediterranean-style façade, waterfall, and fountain.

One of the valley's newest wineries, Culbertson opened in 1988 and has since introduced thousands of visitors to the pleasures of champagne. The winery also operates an on-site bistro called Cafe

Champagne, offering indoor and outdoor seating.

If you're among the many who aren't sure of the difference

between a Brut and Blanc de Noir, following are brief descriptions of some of Culbertson's sparkling wines.

Culbertson's NV Brut is a blend of vintages, and is made from Chardonnay and Pinot Blanc grapes. Vintage Brut Rosé is primarily Pinot Noir with a touch of Chardonnay.

Blanc de Noir is a fruity-tasting, pink-colored champagne that comes primarily from Pinot Noir grapes. Cuvée Rouge is a blend of two different Pinot Noir wines, one part crushed and fermented on the skins and the other part whole-cluster pressed. Cuvée de Frontignan is best enjoyed as a dessert wine or with spicy foods.

By the way, when enjoying a bottle of Culbertson champagne, we suggest that you not use those wide, shallow glasses often used at receptions. In addition to being downright awkward to drink from, they allow bubbles to disappear quickly. In a more appropriate tulip or flute-shaped glass, the champagne retains its bubbles longer.

THE WINE LIST
Blanc de Noir
NV Brut
Vintage Brut
Vintage Brut Reserve
Vintage Brut Rosé
Cuvée Rouge
Cuvée de Frontignan
Vintage Founders Reserve
Vintage Natural

VINTNER'S CHOICES
WHITE: *NV Brut*
RED: *Blanc de Noir*

CULBERTSON WINERY
32575 RANCHO
CALIFORNIA ROAD
TEMECULA, CA 92591
(909) 699-0099

WINERY HOURS: *10 a.m.-5 p.m. daily*
CAFE HOURS: *11 a.m.-9 p.m. daily*
TASTINGS: *Weekends only*
CHARGE FOR TASTING: *Yes*
TOURS: *Weekends on the hour*
PICNIC AREA: *No*
RETAIL SALES: *Yes*

DIRECTIONS: *From Interstate 15, exit east on Rancho California Road and drive four miles to winery on right. Temecula is ninety miles southeast of Los Angeles and sixty miles north of San Diego.*

MOUNT PALOMAR WINERY

Temecula

"*There are fortunes to be made in the winery business,*" *a vintner once confided to us.* "*But it's much easier if you start with a fortune.*"

While Southern California's wine country has its share of entrepreneurs who've spun gold from straw, there are probably more who entered the business after achieving financial success in other businesses. John Poole is among the legion of California vintners who traded lucrative business careers for a winery in the country. Although John's first career, as the owner of radio stations, didn't offer much of a foundation in the wine business, he sold his Los Angeles–based

company and became a self-described "farm boy." His winery, which opened in 1977, was among the Temecula Valley area's first. That was decades ago. Today, the Mount Palomar patriarch is retired, having passed on management responsibilities to his son, Peter.

Visitors are received in the gleaming tile-floored tasting room and gift shop whose walls are festooned with wine ribbons and medals. The wood-and stucco-sided winery is one of the valley's most hospitable, as evidenced by numerous outdoor places to relax. In addition to a covered patio, several picnic tables are scattered about the grounds. Visitors don't even need to pack their own lunch. Mount Palomar's tasting room also offers a deli.

THE WINE LIST
Chardonnay
Extra Dry Champagne
Johannisberg Riesling
Sauvignon Blanc
White Zinfandel
Cabernet Sauvignon
Cream Sherry
Port

VINTNER'S CHOICES
WHITE: *Chardonnay*
RED: *Cabernet Sauvignon*

MOUNT PALOMAR WINERY
33820 RANCHO CALIFORNIA ROAD
TEMECULA, CA 92589
(909) 676-5047

HOURS: *9 a.m.-5 p.m. daily*
TASTINGS: *Yes*
CHARGE FOR TASTING: *Yes*
TOURS: *Yes*
PICNIC AREA: *Yes*
RETAIL SALES: *Yes*

DIRECTIONS: *From Interstate 15, exit east on Rancho California Road and drive five miles to winery on left. Temecula is ninety miles southeast of Los Angeles and sixty miles north of San Diego.*

MAURICE CAR´RIE VINEYARD AND WINERY

Temecula

We dare you to drive by Maurice Car´rie Vineyard and Winery *without stopping. This is undoubtedly one of the most picturesque wineries in all of California, and it lures wine country travelers like Disneyland draws kids.*

The operation is named after Maurice VanRoekel, who with her husband, Budd, created the neo-Victorian farmhouse-style winery from the ground up. Budd and Maurice, who built the Skate Ranch in Orange County, retired to Temecula Valley and established the winery

in 1986, incorporating the ranch vineyards that date back to the 1960s.

While the winery, with its one-hundred-fifty-thousand-gallon capacity, is impressive in its own right, the focal point here is the ornate tasting room, deli, and wine-related gift shop, as well as the expansive grounds, which

THE WINE LIST
Cabernet Blanc
Chardonnay
Chenin Blanc
Heather's Mist white table wine
Johannisberg Riesling
Muscat Canelli
Sauvignon Blanc (Sara Bella)
Sparkling wine
White Zinfandel
Cabernet Sauvignon
Cody's Crush red blend
Pinot Noir

VINTNER'S CHOICES
WHITE: *Reserve Chardonnay*
RED: *Cabernet Sauvignon*

MAURICE CAR´RIE
VINEYARD AND WINERY
34225 RANCHO
CALIFORNIA ROAD
TEMECULA, CA 92591
(909) 676-1711

HOURS: *10 a.m.-5 p.m. daily*
TASTINGS: *Yes*
CHARGE FOR TASTING:
Only for groups of fifteen or more
TOURS: *By appointment*
PICNIC AREA: *Yes*
RETAIL SALES: *Yes*

DIRECTIONS: *From Interstate 15, exit east on Rancho California Road and drive six miles to winery on right. Temecula is ninety miles southeast of Los Angeles and sixty miles north of San Diego.*

even boast a classic gazebo. There's also a play area here to keep the kids happy while mom and dad enjoy a taste.

The eclectic wine list includes a few reasonably priced blends named for family members. Heather's Mist (Heather is the couple's granddaughter) is a blend of Chenin Blanc, Sauvignon Blanc, and Muscat Canelli. Cody's Crush, named after a grandson, combines Merlot, Cabernet Sauvignon, Johannisberg Riesling, and Muscat Canelli.

CILURZO VINEYARD & WINERY

Temecula

In 1967, Emmy Award–winning ABC TV lighting director Vincenzo Cilurzo and his wife, Audrey, set out on a weekend pleasure trip from Hollywood to the Temecula Valley. The couple was so smitten with the destination that they bought a hundred-acre parcel just off Rancho California Road. Their intention was to someday create a retirement retreat, but plans changed when soil and climate test results confirmed the valley's potential for growing wine grapes. By 1968, the Cilurzos were cultivating a forty-acre

premium vineyard—the valley's first. The same year, Audrey gave birth to a daughter whom the couple christened Chenin, after one of the varietals planted. Ten years later Cilurzo Vineyard & Winery was established.

The nondescript winery building won't win any architectural awards, but the homespun and informal interior and hospitable staff make it an enjoyable stop on a wine tour of the region. On one wall hang letters from and photos of many celebrities, including Frank Sinatra and David Letterman, who've worked with Vincenzo and/or sampled his wines. (Letterman's hand-written testament, although not appropriate for this book, is particularly comical.)

At the time of our visit, son Vinnie was doing double-duty as cashier and tasting host. Several folding chairs were set before a small gingham-covered table where various wines were available to sample. The bottling line is visible in an adjacent room.

Vincenzo, the Temecula Valley's wine patriarch, isn't as active in the day-to-day business these days, but he often pops in during weekends to chat with visitors about his show biz career and about Cilurzo wines. Although he'll gladly answer your questions about the luminaries with whom he's worked, don't ask him which wines are his favorite. "That's like asking me which of my children do I love the most," he said.

Among the Cilurzo family wines is a Nouveau Petite Sirah. The uncrushed grapes are placed in bunches in stainless steel tanks and fermentation takes place inside the individual berries. The resulting fruity-tasting wine, available in early fall, is meant to be drunk young.

THE WINE LIST
Chardonnay
Chenin Blanc
Sauvignon Blanc
White Zinfandel
Cabernet Sauvignon
Late Harvest Petite Sirah
Merlot
Muscat Canelli
Nouveau Petite Sirah
Petite Sirah
Vincheno, a red and white blend

VINTNER'S CHOICES
WHITE: *Chenin Blanc*
RED: *Petite Sirah*

CILURZO VINEYARD & WINERY
41220 CALLE CONTENTO
TEMECULA, CA 92592
(909) 676-5250

HOURS: *9:30 a.m.-5 p.m. daily*
TASTINGS: *Yes*
CHARGE FOR TASTING: *Yes; refunded on purchase*
TOURS: *Self-guided*
PICNIC AREA: *Yes*
RETAIL SALES: *Yes*

DIRECTIONS: *From Interstate 15, exit east on Rancho California Road and drive approximately five miles to Calle Contento. Turn right and follow unpaved road to winery on left. Temecula is ninety miles southeast of Los Angeles and sixty miles north of San Diego.*

BAILY VINEYARD AND WINERY

Temecula

There are two ways to get to Baily Vineyard: the high road and the low road. On our first visit we took the high road. Wrong choice! As Phil and Carol Baily so aptly described it, "The dirt road over the hills from Rancho California Road is not in the book of records as the twentieth century's most harrowing experience. It was at one time, but it has been replaced by backpacking from Beirut to Teheran while carrying an American flag." If you plan to visit the Bailys' tidy winery (and we heartily encourage it), do yourselves, and your car, a favor and approach it from the paved low road (see directions).

One of the Temecula Valley's newest wineries—it opened in 1986—Baily is typical of California's mom-and-pop-type operations. Phil,

whose previous occupation was as a computer software developer, works with his wife and partner, Carol, and sons Chris and Pat, to turn out just over three-thousand cases per year. About seven acres here are dedicated to grape growing.

The winery's little cellar can be viewed from the railing along the tasting area. The Baily wine cellar is also the site of several popular dinners held to celebrate the harvest, new releases, the rite of spring, and other occasions.

Those interested in tasting Baily wines without making the trek to the winery may sample the family's wares at a separate tasting room along more heavily traveled Rancho California Road. Baily wines are sold only at the winery and tasting room.

The Bailys are also the proprietors of Baily Wine Country Cafe in the Temecula Town Center, at the corner of Rancho California and Ynez roads near Interstate 15. The wine list includes over fifty varieties. For reservations call (909) 676-9567.

THE WINE LIST
Cabernet Blanc
Chardonnay
Montage, a blend of Sauvignon Blanc and Semillon
Muscat Blanc
Sauvignon Blanc
White Riesling
Cabernet Nouveau
Cabernet Sauvignon

VINTNER'S CHOICES
WHITE: *Montage blend*
RED: *Cabernet Sauvignon*

BAILY VINEYARD AND WINERY
36150 PAUBA ROAD
TEMECULA, CA 92589
TASTING ROOM LOCATION:
33833 RANCHO CALIFORNIA ROAD
(909) 676-WINE

WINERY HOURS: *11 a.m.-5 p.m. Saturday and Sunday*
TASTING ROOM HOURS: *10 a.m.-5 p.m. daily*
TASTINGS: *Yes; both locations; refundable on purchase*
CHARGE FOR TASTING: *Yes; both locations*
TOURS: *At the winery*
PICNIC AREA: *Yes; both locations*
RETAIL SALES: *Yes; both locations*

DIRECTIONS TO WINERY: *From Interstate 15, drive south on Highway 79 for five miles to Anza Road. Turn left on Anza and right on First Street (DePortola). Drive two miles to Pauba Road and turn left. Winery is on the right near the top of the hill.*

DIRECTIONS TO TASTING ROOM: *From Interstate 15, exit east on Rancho California Road and drive five miles to tasting room driveway on right.*

KEYWAYS VINEYARD AND WINERY

Temecula

ike many vintners we meet on California's back roads, Carl Key developed an interest in wine "just as a hobby." But as we've seen, creating fine wines can be as intoxicating as the beverage itself, and Carl is another example of a hobbyist gone wild.

Although a successful career in the restaurant business earned for him the option for a comfortable, easy retirement in the beautiful home he built on a ranch outside Temecula, Carl decided to grow some grapes and build a winery. So much for a relaxing retirement.

The Spanish-style winery and its lush vineyard stand in striking contrast to the barren hillside that rises behind the property. Inside the building, Carl has created an inviting environment for visitors.

The tasting bar is an antique brought from a saloon in old-town Temecula. A restored 1929 Ford is also on display here.

Keyways' growing list of wines includes Misty Key, an interesting blend of Gewürztraminer and Emerald Riesling. The winery also produces Muscat Canelli dessert wine.

For Carl, one of the few disadvantages of running his backcountry winery is a shortage of eligible female visitors. "It's lonely out here," he told us. "I need a wife. Put that in your book."

Keyways' posted days of operation are Friday through Sunday, but visitors may also find the doors open Monday through Thursday when Carl and his staff are working in the winery.

THE WINE LIST
Chardonnay
Misty Key, an Emerald
 Riesling/Gewürztraminer blend
Muscat Canelli
Sauvignon Blanc
White Zinfandel
Cabernet Sauvignon

VINTNER'S CHOICES
WHITE: *Muscat Canelli*
RED: *Cabernet Sauvignon*

KEYWAYS WINERY AND VINEYARD
37338 DEPORTOLA ROAD
TEMECULA, CA 92592
(909) 676-1451

HOURS: *10 a.m.-5 p.m. Friday through Sunday*
TASTINGS: *Yes*
CHARGE FOR TASTING: *Yes*
TOURS: *No*
PICNIC AREA: *Yes*
RETAIL SALES: *Yes*

DIRECTIONS: *From Interstate 15, drive south on Highway 79 for five miles to Anza Road. Turn left on Anza and right on First Street, which becomes DePortola Road. Follow DePortola Road to winery on left.*

FILSINGER VINEYARDS AND WINERY

Temecula

*T*he most remote of Temecula's wineries, Filsinger Vineyards and Winery is situated a few miles east of the valley's largest concentration of winemaking operations. As a consequence of its isolation, Filsinger is among the region's least crowded wineries and best kept secrets.

From the road, the Filsinger winery, with its tiled roof and bell tower, resembles a little California mission. However, the winery's builders opted for white stucco over adobe and plaster.

Open since 1980, the winery was created by Dr. William Filsinger, a family practice physician who practices at nearby Inland Valley Hospital. The Filsinger family built their attractive winery near the center of a thirty-five-acre property, much of it given to vineyards. About eight-thousand cases are produced each year.

Outside the winery is a gazebo, which shades a few picnic tables. A small tasting area also holds gift items.

THE WINE LIST
Brut Champagne
Brut Rosé Champagne
Chardonnay
Extra Dry Champagne
Fumé Blanc
Gewürztraminer
Johannisberg Riesling
White Zinfandel
Cabernet Sauvignon
Gamay Beaujolais

VINTNER'S CHOICES
WHITE: *Gewürztraminer*
RED: *Cabernet Sauvignon*

FILSINGER VINEYARDS AND WINERY
39050 DE PORTOLA ROAD
TEMECULA, CA 92390
(909) 676-4594

HOURS: *By appointment, weekdays; 10:30 a.m.-5 p.m. Saturday and Sunday*
TASTINGS: *Yes*
CHARGE FOR TASTING: *Yes*
TOURS: *By appointment*
PICNIC AREA: *Yes*
RETAIL SALES: *Yes*

DIRECTIONS: *From Interstate 15, drive south on Highway 79 for five miles to Anza Road. Turn left on Anza and right on First Street, which becomes DePortola Road. Follow DePortola Road to winery on left, past Keyways Vineyard and Winery. From Rancho California Road wineries, continue east to Glenoaks Road. Turn right and follow to De Portola Road. Turn right and follow to winery on right.*

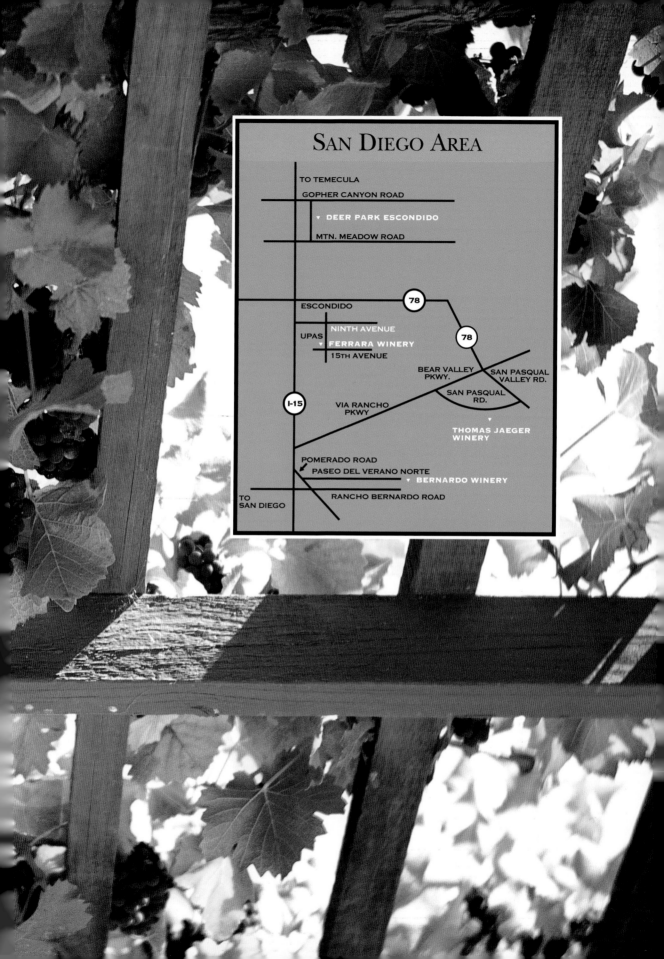

DEER PARK ESCONDIDO

Escondido

*W*e've heard of remote wineries establishing tasting rooms a few miles nearer to the main road, but in Deer Park's case, the tasting room was built six-hundred miles away.

Deer Park Escondido was conceived by Bob and Lila Knapp to showcase both the couple's vintage auto collection and wines produced at Napa Valley's Deer Park Winery, co-owned by the Knapps with David and Kinta Clark. Then in 1981, soon after buying the Escondido property, Bob and Lila planted a three-acre plot of Chardonnay grapes, ignoring skeptics who claimed the hot and dry climate was ill-suited to the somewhat delicate varietal. Cooled by marine breezes, the microclimate of the little vineyard, located on the valley floor near a creek, turned out to be a pleasant surprise. The

first crop, harvested in 1985, was trucked six-hundred miles north to Deer Park Winery in the hills above St. Helena. Under the direction of David Clark, grapes were crushed and fermented and the wine was barrel-aged, bottled, and then trucked back to Escondido for bottle-aging and ultimately for sale.

Impressed with the potential of their Escondido Chardonnay, the partners decided it would be much easier to produce the wine closer to home and shuttle the winemaker between the two sites. Thus, a "miniwinery" was built,

with all the equipment needed to produce up to six-hundred cases per year.

Sharing the mission-style winery building is a Fifties auto collection as well as displays of vintage bicycles, Barbie dolls, radios, and baby buggies. A short stroll away is yet another building housing an even larger antique car collection. The Knapps boast the world's largest collection of American convertibles. Also on the estate is a tasting room, deli, and gift shop.

At harvest time, typically in late August, the winery invites the public to watch grapes being crushed in a vintage wine press and to taste fresh Chardonnay juice. The Escondido Chardonnay is sold here along with wines from Deer Park Winery north.

By the way, fans of Lawrence Welk will be pleased to know the winery is next to Lawrence Welk Village.

THE WINE LIST
Escondido Chardonnay
Fumé Blush
Sauvignon Blanc
Cabernet Sauvignon
Petite Sirah
Zinfandel

VINTNER'S CHOICES
WHITE: *Chardonnay*
RED: *Petite Sirah*

**DEER PARK ESCONDIDO
29013 CHAMPAGNE
BOULEVARD
ESCONDIDO, CA 92026
(619) 749-1666**

HOURS: *10 a.m.-5 p.m. daily; auto museum open 10 a.m.-4 p.m. daily*
TASTINGS: *Yes*
CHARGE FOR TASTING: *No*
**CHARGE FOR AUTO
MUSEUM TOUR:** *Yes*
TOURS: *Self-guided*
PICNIC AREA: *Yes*
RETAIL SALES: *Yes*

DIRECTIONS: *From Interstate 15, take the Deer Springs Road/Mountain Meadow exit and drive east to Champagne Boulevard (old Highway 395). Turn left and drive to winery on right.*

BERNARDO WINERY

San Diego

*W*e came looking for San Diego County's oldest winery. What we found was one of the southland's most unusual specialty shopping plazas whose centerpiece is a veritable wine museum. A gift shop, arts and crafts boutiques, and a clothing store are among the offerings in the old Bernardo Winery compound. Some of the buildings here date back to 1889, the year the winery was established. There are even a few acres of century-old vines still being tended.

The winery and tasting room comprise one corner of the property. Crammed with an intriguing assortment of farming and winemaking relics, it's also the most interesting part. Instead of taking a formal tour, visitors are free to poke around the place. The hulking redwood vats, concrete fermenting tanks, timeworn wine presses, and walls laden with antique farming bric-a-brac make for an entertaining diversion.

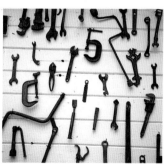

After the self-guided history lesson in winemaking most visitors head for the tasting room, where about two-dozen different wines are sold. You'll also find gift items, as well as Bernardo olive oil, wine sauces, and jellies and jams.

In addition to serving as the shopping plaza's landlord, Bernardo Winery owner Ross Rizzo still finds time to create eight-to-ten-thousand gallons of wine each year, using the same traditional methods employed by his winemaking father. The Rizzo family has owned the property since 1928.

THE WINE LIST
Chablis
Chardonnay
Chenin Blanc
French Colombard
Gewürztraminer
Johannisberg Riesling
White Zinfandel
Burgundy
Cabernet Sauvignon
Napa Gamay
Vin Rosé
Vino di Rosario
Dessert wines
Fruit wines

VINTNER'S CHOICES
WHITE: *Chardonnay*
RED: *Cabernet Sauvignon*

BERNARDO WINERY
13330 PASEO DEL VERANO
NORTE
SAN DIEGO, CA 92128
(619) 487-1866

HOURS: *9 a.m.-5 p.m. daily*
TASTINGS: *Yes*
CHARGE FOR TASTING: *No*
TOURS: *Self-guided*
PICNIC AREA: *Reserved for parties*
RETAIL SALES: *Yes*

DIRECTIONS: *From Interstate 15, exit at Rancho Bernardo Road and drive east. Turn left on Pomerado Road and right on Paseo del Verano. Drive one-and-a-half miles to winery sign.*

FERRARA WINERY

Escondido

A once-thriving wine industry has been among the victims of San Diego County's hungry suburban sprawl. As the region's population has blossomed, acres and acres of vineyards have gradually been replaced by neighborhoods and malls. Ferrara Winery is among only a couple of the region's original wineries that have survived the growth. A state historical point of interest, this winemaking landmark is a must-see for wine and history buffs. Although its vineyards have over the years been squeezed to about five remaining acres, there's still much to experience here.

Little appears to have changed at the winery since the late George Ferrara established the business in 1932. The winery buildings look their age, and pieces of retired winemaking equipment dot the

grounds. The Ferrara family is still running the show, although George's son, Gasper, is now in charge. When we dropped by, Gasper, born and raised here, was pouring samples for visitors in the dimly lit tasting room, whose shelves are lined with jugs of what he described as "good everyday wine." Visitors may also buy sandwiches here.

Although tight-lipped about his personal favorites, Gasper is obviously proud of an ancient three-acre vineyard of Muscat of Alexandria, among the last remaining plots of what used to be one of San Diego's most famous grapes. It's now grown widely in the San Joaquin Valley for raisins.

The Ferraras maintain a quaint roofed picnic area with tables covered by gingham cloths. Nearby, several photos depict the winemaking process, which can be viewed from a distance.

Ferrara Winery produces about one-hundred-thousand gallons each year.

THE WINE LIST

Ferrara produces a lengthy selection of premium varietals, jug wines, blends, dessert wines, specialty wines, grape juice, wine marinade, and wine vinegar.

FERRARA WINERY
1120 WEST FIFTEENTH
AVENUE
ESCONDIDO, CA 92025
(619) 745-7632

HOURS: *9 a.m.-5:30 p.m. Monday through Friday; 10 a.m.-5:30 p.m. Saturday and Sunday*
TASTINGS: *Yes*
CHARGE FOR TASTING: *No*
TOURS: *No*
PICNIC AREA: *Yes*
RETAIL SALES: *Yes*

DIRECTIONS: *From Interstate 15 in Escondido, exit at Ninth Avenue and drive east to Upas Avenue. Turn right and drive to Fifteenth Avenue. Turn right and drive to winery on right.*

THOMAS JAEGER WINERY

Escondido

*W*hile the winemaker's goal—to produce high quality wine—
hasn't changed in San Diego's century of winemaking, the
technology has advanced by leaps and bounds. For an eye-popping
trip through the ages of winemaking, we suggest you follow a tour of
Escondido's old wooden wineries, described in the previous pages,
with a visit to nearby Thomas Jaeger, San Diego's largest state-of-the-
art premium winery.

Originally known as the San Pasqual Winery, the enterprise was res-
cued from bankruptcy in 1987 by Paul Thomas of San Diego and Bill

Jaeger, a partner in Napa Valley's Freemark Abbey and Rutherford Hill wineries. After renaming the winery, the partners set about creating a fresh image based on innovation and improvements. In 1992 Thomas Jaeger

unveiled San Diego's first Merlot to excellent reviews, and General Manager Leon Santoro undertook an experimental grafting of Chardonnay vines with other varietals including Sangiovese, a classical Italian grape not common to these parts.

The partners' cavernous warehouse-sized winery dominates a high spot overlooking much of San Pasqual Valley. The thirty-acre estate vineyard is complemented by a leased sixty-acre plot in Fallbrook. About fourteen-thousand cases of Thomas Jaeger wine are produced each year.

Picnic tables beneath a grape arbor offer sweeping views of the vineyard and rugged San Pasqual Valley. An adjacent grassy expanse called Rose Park is also open to winery visitors. In addition to wine, the large tasting room here sells picnic foods and gift items.

THE WINE LIST
Chardonnay
Gewürztraminer
Johannisberg Riesling
Muscat Canelli
White Zinfandel
Cabernet Sauvignon
Merlot
Zinfandel Port

VINTNER'S CHOICES
WHITE: *Chardonnay*
RED: *Merlot*

THOMAS JAEGER WINERY
13455 SAN PASQUAL ROAD
ESCONDIDO, CA 92925
(619) 745-3553

HOURS: *10 a.m.-6 p.m. daily*
TASTINGS: *Yes*
CHARGE FOR TASTING: *No*
TOURS: *Yes*
PICNIC AREA: *Yes*
RETAIL SALES: *Yes*

DIRECTIONS: *From Interstate 15 south of Escondido, exit at Via Rancho Parkway, following signs to the San Diego Wild Animal Park. Turn right on San Pasqual Road and drive one mile to the winery entrance on right.*

*A Guide to Some Nontraditional Wines
of the Back Roads*

On any backroad winery tour, you'll find plenty of the famous fine varietals that have placed California on the wine map. But along with Cabernet and Chardonnay you'll encounter wine lists with less familiar names, like Roussanne, Vernaccia, Pinot Gris, and Sangiovese.

On Southern California's back roads we met a number of vintners who are stepping outside traditional enological boundaries by working with grapes rarely—if ever—used by other Golden State winemakers. Since California's backcountry vintners represent the driving force behind this trend, tasters willing to bring something a bit new and different home to the dinner table will discover some true finds.

Just so you're not tasting in the dark, following is a brief listing of a few grapes whose names may be unfamiliar.

ALEATICO

A Southern Italian grape, the wine from which is light red in color and full of flavor, somewhat similar to that of Muscat. Martin Brothers Winery in Paso Robles produces Aleatico.

BOUCHET

Also known as Cabernet Franc

CARMINE

Carmine is a hybrid cross between Ruby Cabernet and Merlot. Mastantuono Winery in Templeton uses these grapes to create Carminello, a deep red wine with pronounced flavors.

FUMÉ BLANC

Fumé Blanc and Sauvignon Blanc may be used interchangeably. Sometimes Fumé Blanc connotes a drier and/or "oaky" version of Sauvignon Blanc.

GAMAY BEAUJOLAIS

This wine isn't particularly unusual in California; however, many are unaware that it's a clone of Pinot Noir. Fuller-bodied examples of Gamay Beaujolais are often called Pinot Noir.

MALVASIA

The white Malvasia is commonly used as a blending grape to create Chianti made in Italy's Tuscany region.

MARSANNE

See Roussanne

MOURVÈDRE

Mourvèdre, popular in France, has only recently been rediscovered by California winemakers. The taste has been likened to blackberry and anise. Hart Winery in Temecula makes Mourvèdre.

MUSCAT CANELLI

This grape, sometimes referred to as Muscat Blanc or Muscat Frontignan, makes a sweet white sipping or dessert wine that is gaining in popularity. A number of Southern California wineries, including Hope Farms, Maurice Car´rie Winery, and Mission View Estate, produce Muscat Canelli.

NEBBIOLO

The grape from which Italian Barolo and Barbaresco wines are made thrives in districts where morning fog is often present during the growing season. Martin Brothers Winery in Paso Robles specializes in this unusual wine, whose descriptors include mushrooms, cedar, violets, and black currants. Justin Vineyards and Winery and Arciero Winery, both in Paso Robles, market this wine as well.

PETIT VERDOT

Bordeaux winemakers commonly use this grape in blending; a few California backroad wineries have begun to incorporate it in Cabernet Sauvignon.

PINOT BLANC

You'll notice the similarity of this wine to Chardonnay; Pinot Blanc has a more subtle, tart taste.

ROUSSANNE

Roussanne, often blended with Marsanne, is finding its way into white California wines made in the style of the Rhône region of France.

SANGIOVESE

This is the primary red variety of Italy's famous northern Chianti district.

SAUVIGNON BLANC

See Fumé Blanc

SEMILLON

Traditionally blended with Sauvignon Blanc as a softener, this white grape produces a light and fruity wine that's being produced on its own by a growing number of vintners. The wine is also occasionally called Chevrier. Baily Vineyard and Winery in Temecula makes a gold medal–winning dry Montage that's about sixty-percent Sauvignon Blanc and about forty-percent Semillon.

VERNACCIA

This is a Tuscan grape that makes a dry white wine.

VIOGNIER

One of America's largest plantings of this increasingly popular white grape is located on the central coast of California. Viognier wines, which hail from France's Rhône Valley, have wide-ranging aromas that include honeysuckle, peach, and orange blossom.

WINE ROAD RESOURCES

Romantic Inns and Small Hotels

THE MONTEREY COUNTY REGION

Ventana
Highway 1
Big Sur
(408) 667-2331

Tickle Pink
155 Highland Drive
Carmel
(408) 624-1244

Mission Ranch
26270 Dolores Street
Carmel
(408) 624-6436

THE PASO ROBLES AND SAN LUIS OBISPO AREAS

Just Inn at Justin Vineyards and Winery
11680 Chimney Rock Road
Paso Robles
(805) 238-6932

Baywood Bed and Breakfast Inn
1370 Second Street
Baywood Park
(805) 528-8888

Garden Street Inn
1212 Garden Street
San Luis Obispo
(805) 545-9802

Blue Whale Inn
6736 Moonstone Beach Drive
Cambria
(805) 927-4647

SANTA YNEZ VALLEY AND VENTURA

Los Olivos Grand Hotel
2860 Grand Avenue
Los Olivos
(805) 688-7788

Ballard Inn (pictured here)
2436 Baseline Road
Ballard
(805) 688-7770

La Mer
411 Poli Street
Ventura
(805) 643-3600

TEMECULA

Temecula Creek Inn
44501 Rainbow Canyon Road
Temecula
(909) 694-1000 or 676-5631

THE SAN DIEGO AREA

The Bed-and-Breakfast Inn at La Jolla
7753 Draper Avenue
La Jolla
(619) 456-2066

Pelican Cove Inn
320 Walnut Avenue
Carlsbad
(619) 434-5995

Rancho Bernardo Inn
17550 Bernardo Oaks Drive
San Diego
(619) 487-1611

Recommended Restaurants

THE MONTEREY COUNTY REGION

Crayons Wine Bar and Restaurant
172 Main Street
Salinas
(408) 759-9355

Carmel Valley Ranch Resort
1 Old Ranch Road
Carmel Valley
(408) 625-9500

Rio Grill
Crossroads Center
Rio Road and Highway One
Carmel
(408) 625-5436

THE PASO ROBLES AND SAN LUIS OBISPO AREAS

Berardi and Sons
1202 Pine Street
Paso Robles
(805) 238-1330

Cafe Roma
1819 Osos Street
San Luis Obispo
(805) 541-6800

Buono Tavola
1037 Monterey Street
San Luis Obispo
(805) 545-8000

The Sow's Ear Cafe
2248 Main Street
Cambria
(805) 927-4865

THE SANTA BARBARA AREA

Los Olivos Grand Hotel Restaurant
2860 Grand Avenue
Los Olivos
(805) 688-7788

Hitching Post
3325 Point Sal Road
Casmalia (near Los Olivos)
(805) 937-6151

Mattei's Tavern
Highway 154
Los Olivos
(805) 688-4820

El Encanto Hotel Dining Room
1900 Lasuen Road
Santa Barbara
(805) 967-5000

TEMECULA

Temecula Creek Inn
44501 Rainbow Canyon Road
Temecula
(909) 694-1000 or 676-5631

Baily Wine Country Cafe
27644 Ynez Road
Temecula
(909) 676-9567

Cafe Champagne at Culbertson Winery
32575 Rancho California Road
Temecula
(909) 699-0088

THE SAN DIEGO AREA

El Bizcocho at Rancho Bernardo Inn
17550 Bernardo Oaks Drive
San Diego
(619) 487-1611

The Winesellar and Brasserie
9550 Waples Street
San Diego
(619) 450-9557

Elario's
7955 La Jolla Shores Drive
La Jolla
(619) 459-0541

Primo Picnic Grounds

Following, by region, are wineries whose picnic areas are highly recommended. All had picnic tables at the time of our visit. We suggest (and some establishments stipulate)

that you follow backroad winery etiquette and not open wine from another winery during your picnic. These picnic areas are for winery visitors only. Most sell chilled wines. Refer to winery entries for directions.

THE MONTEREY COUNTY REGION

Cloninger Cellars—shaded, with farmland views

Chalone Vineyard—under oak trees with vineyard views

THE PASO ROBLES AND SAN LUIS OBISPO AREAS

Hope Farms—gazebo and lawn, plus a deli

Meridian Vineyards—under the oaks with vineyard views

Martin Brothers Winery—vineyard views

Arciero Winery—outdoors or indoors, plus a deli

Talley Vineyards—vineyard views

THE SANTA YNEZ VALLEY

Carey Cellars—on a deck with vineyard views

Zaca Mesa Winery—under the oaks

The Gainey Vineyard—vineyard views

THE TEMECULA VALLEY

Mount Palomar Winery—tables numerous, with winery and vineyard views, plus gourmet foods and sandwiches for sale

Maurice Car'rie Vineyard and Winery—local views plus deli

Baily Vineyard and Winery—valley views

Filsinger Vineyards—covered deck with vineyard views

THE SAN DIEGO AREA

Thomas Jaeger Winery—grassy park and grape arbors with valley views, plus gourmet foods for sale

Deer Park Escondido—three scenic park areas plus a deli

BACKROAD WINE TOUR MAPS

Free color maps that include updated regional listings of wineries, along with locations, hours, and services, are available at tasting rooms of member wineries, or from the following vintner organizations:

Monterey Wine Country Associates
P.O. Box 1793
Monterey, CA 93942
(408) 375-9400

Paso Robles Chamber of Commerce
548 Spring Street
Paso Robles, CA 93446
(805) 238-0506

Edna Valley Arroyo Grande Valley Vintners
P.O. Box 159
Arroyo Grande, CA 93420
(805) 541-5868

Santa Barbara County Vintners' Association
P.O. Box 1558
Santa Ynez, CA 93460-1558
(805) 688-0881

Temecula Valley Vintners Association
P.O. Box 1601
Temecula, CA 92593-1601
(909) 699-3626

Index

NOTES